MAKING CHOICES

A Personal Look at Alcohol & Drug Use

Marjorie E. Scaffa
University of Maryland

Sandra C. Quinn
University of Maryland

Robert A. Swift
University of Maryland

WCB Wm. C. Brown Publishers

Book Team

Editor *Chris Rogers*
Developmental Editor *Susan McCormick*
Production Coordinator *Peggy Selle*

WCB **Wm. C. Brown Publishers**

President *G. Franklin Lewis*
Vice President, Publisher *Thomas E. Doran*
Vice President, Operations and Production *Beverly Kolz*
National Sales Manager *Virginia S. Moffat*
Group Sales Manager *John Finn*
Executive Editor *Edgar J. Laube*
Director of Marketing *Kathy Law Laube*
Marketing Manager *George H. Chapin*
Managing Editor, Production *Colleen A. Yonda*
Manager of Visuals and Design *Faye M. Shilling*
Production Editorial Manager *Julie A. Kennedy*
Production Editorial Manager *Ann Fuerste*
Publishing Services Manager *Karen J. Slaght*

WCB Group

President and Chief Executive Officer *Mark C. Falb*
Chairman of the Board *Wm. D. Brown*

Cover design by Sailer & Cook Creative Services
Illustration Patti Green
Copyedited by Kathy P. Anderson

TABLE OF CONTENTS

TO THE INSTRUCTOR

It has been our experience that many students who choose to enroll in an elective alcohol and drug course do so for personal reasons. Typically, a fair percentage are experimenting with drugs, and most are drinking frequently, often to excess. In addition, a large number of students are dealing with the chemical abuse or chemical dependence of a close friend or family member. For these reasons, we strongly believe that an affective component to traditionally cognitively oriented college drug and alcohol classes is essential. This workbook is an attempt to fill that need.

The workbook also fulfills a need for us as instructors. It can function as a needs-assessment tool through which you can determine the class' needs and tailor course content appropriately. It allows for personal, yet private, communication between students and faculty members and can serve as an opportunity to screen students for alcohol and drug-related problems and make appropriate referrals. We have found that the level of disclosure in these exercises is often quite profound. Therefore, it is appropriate and necessary, at the outset, to assure students of their confidentiality and the availability and willingness of the instructor to discuss these issues in private, should the student so desire.

Many of the exercises may be useful in stimulating small-group discussions, and in some cases, class means and ranges can be calculated so students can find out where they stand on various issues with respect to their peers.

We hope this workbook enhances your students' understanding and ability to effectively deal with alcohol and other drug problems on a personal level, in relationships, and on a societal level. We also hope this workbook enhances your ability to communicate with your students in a more meaningful way about these issues and that you derive satisfaction from knowing you have provided them with more than just facts and information.

If you have any questions or concerns about the use of this workbook, suggestions on future revisions, or want to share your successes with us, please do not hesitate to contact us. We would be delighted to hear from you. Good Luck!

TO THE STUDENT

It has been our experience as instructors that when soliciting opinions on how to make a drug and alcohol course more effective, most students have expressed a desire to explore how they *feel* about themselves and alcohol and other drug issues rather than just be provided with the standard information included in most drug textbooks. Thus, we created a workbook that allows you to do precisely that. You may want to consider the following points as you progress through this workbook:

1) It is probably best to use a pencil with most of the exercises in this workbook. Some of them require decision making that can result in a person changing their response quite a few times.

2) Although the workbook could be used by itself, there may be an accompanying textbook which would provide additional insight or answers to questions.

3) Many of the exercises are self-assessments of knowledge, attitudes, and behaviors. These will change over time, so you may want to complete some of the exercises again, at a later date, to ascertain whether or not your knowledge, attitudes, or behaviors have changed.

4) While this book is intended for use in your classroom, you may want to share some or all of the exercises with your family or friends, when you feel it is appropriate.

When completing the exercises in *Making Choices*, keep in mind that what you learn about yourself is not absolute, but an estimation of your thoughts and feelings about yourself and how these influence the use of alcohol and other drugs in your life. We hope you will use the information you acquire to enhance and support what you already know or to spark you to take further action if you feel it is warranted. Above all, just remember: the choices you make are your own!

ACKNOWLEDGEMENTS

Life is constantly full of challenges, and the writing of this workbook proved to be no exception. Many special people along the way, however, made our work easier and more enjoyable, and for this we are extremely grateful.

Many thanks to:

- our students, who, by their reactions to these exercises in class, gave us encouragement to pursue this project and constructive feedback that guided our revisions;

- our colleagues who tested these materials in their classes;

- Glen G. Gilbert, Chair of the Department of Health Education, University of Maryland, for his enthusiastic support and guidance;

- Chris Rogers at William C. Brown Publishers, for his confidence and willingness to work with three fledgling authors; and to

- Sandra L. Walter, our layout/design consultant, for her creativity, hard work, and tolerance of our unrealistic time lines.

OVERVIEW

This workbook focuses on self-assessment and personal-exploration exercises, structured to examine knowledge, attitudes, and behaviors related to alcohol and other drug use on three levels. The first level addresses personal issues, such as what students think, what they believe, how they feel, and what they do, relative to their personal alcohol and drug use. The second level addresses concerns relative to family members and friends, such as the impact of an addicted parent on the family, how to identify chemical dependence in a family member or friend, and what to do if someone close to the student needs help. The third level addresses alcohol and drug issues on the college campus itself, in the local community, and in society at large.

Each level has two sections. The first section is made up of assessments that force the students to evaluate their knowledge, attitudes, and behavior. The second section follows up with skill-building exercises designed to increase awareness and develop attitudes and behaviors conducive to a healthy lifestyle. This two-step approach acknowledges that, in drug and alcohol education, information by itself is insufficient. Behavioral change requires an exploration of affective components and the development of skills.

This workbook, which could serve as a companion to a traditional text in a drug education class, is designed to meet several needs. Due to its emphasis on self-assessment and personal-exploration exercises, it provides an affective learning component to traditionally cognitively oriented classes. For large classes, it also provides an opportunity for interaction and feedback between students and faculty. Finally, this workbook functions as a private and personal outlet for students to discuss their concerns about alcohol and drug use.

WHAT IS YOUR DRUG AND ALCOHOL IQ?

HOW AWARE ARE YOU OF YOUR FEELINGS REGARDING YOUR OWN ALCOHOL AND DRUG USE?

At present, many people feel that our society is in the midst of a drug epidemic. At the very least, drug and alcohol use — whether legal or not — has become a rather commonplace occurrence in our society. Before assessing alcohol and drug use on a societal level, however, one needs to examine personal knowledge, attitudes, beliefs, and use of licit as well as illicit drugs.

This first section of the workbook takes a look at personal issues surrounding alcohol and drug use at the individual level. No right or wrong beliefs are proclaimed; rather, you are encouraged to formulate your own judgments based on your knowledge, attitudes, and values.

The personal-issues segment begins with a self-assessment, first describing the physical effects of alcohol and drugs on the body, followed by facts about alcohol and drug use. Helpful exercises such as the stress checklist and leisure-interest checklist will enable you to assess factors leading to substance use. The assessments in this chapter are intended to provide you with a reference point from which to begin further exploration into why and when one uses or abstains from alcohol or other drugs.

From the self-assessment, you can progress into the skill-building exercises, which will help you make decisions about alcohol and drug issues based upon your personal knowledge, attitudes, and values. When making personally relevant decisions, most people feel better about themselves, and this satisfaction is usually apparent in one's actions. Exercises in the skill-building segment range from computing your own blood alcohol concentration to assessing your ability to discriminate between responsible vs. irresponsible use, as well as identifying levels of risk-taking behavior. The latter segment of skill building deals with improving decision-making skills and coping strategies, followed lastly by an exploration of alternative means of getting high.

A PERSONAL PORTRAIT

In today's world, alcohol and drugs present many of us with difficult decisions and challenging situations. We are bombarded with information about their use from a variety of sources including family, friends, the media, school, and health care professionals. However, sometimes our knowledge base may contain myths and misinformation. Our attitudes and beliefs about alcohol and drugs stem from our experiences, values, families, and friends. Yet, we may have never identified or articulated our attitudes in a clear way. Finally, our behavior is impacted by our knowledge, attitudes, values, moods, and other factors. For some of us, our behavior may actually conflict with our knowledge about alcohol and drugs and the beliefs we profess to hold.

In this section, you will have the opportunity to explore your knowledge and attitudes about alcohol and drugs, and your alcohol and drug-related behavior. By doing these exercises you will be able to: 1) assess your level of knowledge and determine if you have accurate information, 2) identify your attitudes and values so that you will be able to "own" them, and 3) evaluate your alcohol and drug-related behavior. This growing self-awareness can provide the basis for future decision making regarding alcohol and drug use.

PHYSICAL EFFECTS OF ALCOHOL USE

This test has 20 statements about the possible effects of alcohol use. Put a checkmark to show whether you think each sentence is **TRUE** or **FALSE**. If you don't know whether a sentence is true or false, put a checkmark under **DON'T KNOW**.

TRUE	FALSE	DON'T KNOW		
( )	( )	( )	1.	A person cannot get as drunk by drinking beer as one could by drinking hard liquor.
( )	( )	( )	2.	Frequent drinkers need less alcohol to get drunk than occasional drinkers.
( )	( )	( )	3.	Males can become sexually impotent as a result of regular heavy drinking.
( )	( )	( )	4.	Most people would be considered legally drunk after having four drinks in an hour.
( )	( )	( )	5.	Heavy drinking over a long period of time destroys brain cells.
( )	( )	( )	6.	Alcohol mixed with carbonated soda is less intoxicating than drinking the same amount of alcohol straight.
( )	( )	( )	7.	The effects of alcohol will be the same whether or not a person eats food before drinking.
( )	( )	( )	8.	A person's chance of developing cancer is not affected by drinking.
( )	( )	( )	9.	Frequent heavy drinking often leads to stomach problems.
( )	( )	( )	10.	Regular heavy drinking increases a person's chance of developing heart disease.
( )	( )	( )	11.	Drinking alcohol slows down parts of the brain.
( )	( )	( )	12.	A pregnant woman who drinks is as likely to have a healthy baby as a pregnant woman who does not drink.
( )	( )	( )	13.	Regular heavy drinking increases a person's chance of developing pneumonia.

TRUE	FALSE	DON'T KNOW		
( )	( )	( )	14.	About 75% of people who drink heavily develop liver problems.
( )	( )	( )	15.	Hard liquor has fewer calories than the same amount of a soft drink.
( )	( )	( )	16.	Regular heavy drinking increases a person's chance of having a stroke.
( )	( )	( )	17.	A person who weighs 150 pounds will get just as high on three drinks as a person who weighs 100 pounds.
( )	( )	( )	18.	Drinking coffee is a good way to sober up.
( )	( )	( )	19.	A person cannot become as dependent on alcohol as on heroin.
( )	( )	( )	20.	Frequent heavy drinking often leads to a shortage of vitamins in the body.

SCORING AND ANALYSIS

The answer key for the questionnaire is provided below:

Item No.	Correct Answer
1	F
2	F
3	T
4	T
5	T
6	F
7	F
8	F
9	T
10	T
11	T
12	F
13	T
14	T
15	F
16	T
17	F
18	F
19	F
20	T

This assessment should be scored by counting the number of correct answers. Items marked **"Don't Know"** or left blank should be scored as incorrect.

Number Correct	Rating
18 or greater	Excellent
16-17	Very Good
14-15	Good
12-13	Fair
Less than 12	Poor

SOURCE: Adapted from *Program Evaluation Handbook: Alcohol Abuse Education* (1988). Centers for Disease Control and The Office of Disease Prevention and Health Promotion, U.S. Department of Health and Human Services.

PHYSICAL CONSEQUENCES OF DRUG USE

This test consists of 15 statements about the consequences of drug use. Put a checkmark to show whether you think each statement is **TRUE** or **FALSE**. If you don't know whether a statement is true or false, put a checkmark under **DON'T KNOW**.

TRUE	FALSE	DON'T KNOW		
( )	( )	( )	1.	Cocaine ("coke" or "crack") can produce feelings of extreme anxiety.
( )	( )	( )	2.	Smoking marijuana ("pot," "grass") does not usually interfere with a person's ability to drive a car.
( )	( )	( )	3.	Over time, marijuana ("pot," "grass") users must often smoke more and more marijuana in order to get high to the same degree.
( )	( )	( )	4.	Using a lot of cocaine ("coke" or "crack") over a short period of time can lead to depression.
( )	( )	( )	5.	Smoking crack (cocaine) cannot produce symptoms of cocaine addiction.
( )	( )	( )	6.	A person must take barbiturates ("downers," "reds") for a long period of time before needing to take a greater quantity of the drug in order to feel the desired effect.
( )	( )	( )	7.	One reaction to smoking marijuana ("pot," "grass") is a feeling of panic.
( )	( )	( )	8.	Heavy marijuana ("pot," "grass") use has no negative effects on the throat or lungs.
( )	( )	( )	9.	Regular, low-dose amphetamine ("uppers," "speed") users can develop a psychological need for the drug.
( )	( )	( )	10.	People who smoke cigarettes inhale about 1,500 chemicals into their lungs.
( )	( )	( )	11.	It is easy for a person to control the effects of PCP ("angel dust").
( )	( )	( )	12.	Sharing drug needles is a common way to get the AIDS virus.

TRUE	FALSE	DON'T KNOW		
( )	( )	( )	13.	In small doses, alcohol stimulates the brain.
( )	( )	( )	14.	Methaqualone ("quaaludes," "ludes") is safer than other barbiturate drugs ("downers," "reds") because a person cannot become dependent upon it.
( )	( )	( )	15.	Using shared needles to inject drugs can result in serious blood disease.

SCORING AND ANALYSIS

The answer key for the questionnaire is provided below:

Item No.	Correct Answer
1	T
2	F
3	T
4	T
5	F
6	F
7	T
8	F
9	T
10	T
11	F
12	T
13	F
14	F
15	T

This assessment should be scored by counting the number of correct answers. Items marked "**Don't Know**" or left blank should be scored as incorrect.

Number Correct	Rating
14 or greater	Excellent
12-13	Good
10-11	Fair
Less than 10	Poor

SOURCE: Adapted from *Program Evaluation Handbook: Drug Abuse Education* (1988). Centers for Disease Control and the Office of Disease Prevention and Health Promotion, U.S. Department of Health and Human Services.

IDEAS ABOUT ALCOHOL USE

The sentences below are about how you might be affected by drinking alcohol. Put a checkmark to show how much you agree or disagree with each sentence.

		Strongly Agree	Agree	Not Sure	Disagree	Strongly Disagree
1.	People enjoy being around me more when I've had a few drinks.	( )	( )	( )	( )	( )
2.	I can have a few drinks without my driving being affected.	( )	( )	( )	( )	( )
3.	Alcohol helps me get through stressful situations.	( )	( )	( )	( )	( )
4.	Drinking changes my personality for the worse.	( )	( )	( )	( )	( )
5.	Drinking regularly could result in my becoming addicted to alcohol.	( )	( )	( )	( )	( )
6.	Drinking alcohol is bad for my health.	( )	( )	( )	( )	( )
7.	I could have family problems if I drank alcohol every day.	( )	( )	( )	( )	( )
8.	I have more fun at social events when I drink.	( )	( )	( )	( )	( )
9.	Alcohol has been a negative influence in my life.	( )	( )	( )	( )	( )
10.	My friendships would be damaged if I drank a lot.	( )	( )	( )	( )	( )
11.	I feel more confident when I drink alcohol.	( )	( )	( )	( )	( )

		Strongly Agree	Agree	Not Sure	Disagree	Strongly Disagree
12.	Drinking alcohol is a good way for me to relax and loosen up.	( )	( )	( )	( )	( )
13.	I would feel ashamed if I drank too much.	( )	( )	( )	( )	( )
14.	I would have problems at work if I drank more than I do now.	( )	( )	( )	( )	( )
15.	I would have lower grades in school if I drank more than I do now.	( )	( )	( )	( )	( )
16.	Drinking is a good way to forget my problems.	( )	( )	( )	( )	( )
17.	It is okay if I get drunk once in awhile.	( )	( )	( )	( )	( )
18.	I feel that driving a car after having a few drinks is a stupid thing to do.	( )	( )	( )	( )	( )
19.	I would feel more popular if I drank alcohol.	( )	( )	( )	( )	( )
20.	Drinking alcohol is a normal part of the college experience.	( )	( )	( )	( )	( )

SCORING AND ANALYSIS

Point values are assigned to response options as follows:

Item No.	Strongly Agree	Agree	Not Sure	Disagree	Strongly Disagree
1	1	2	3	4	5
2	1	2	3	4	5
3	1	2	3	4	5
4	5	4	3	2	1
5	5	4	3	2	1
6	5	4	3	2	1
7	5	4	3	2	1
8	1	2	3	4	5
9	5	4	3	2	1
10	5	4	3	2	1
11	1	2	3	4	5
12	1	2	3	4	5
13	5	4	3	2	1
14	5	4	3	2	1
15	5	4	3	2	1
16	1	2	3	4	5
17	1	2	3	4	5
18	5	4	3	2	1
19	1	2	3	4	5
20	1	2	3	4	5

This inventory should be scored by adding the point values of the responses from all of the questions and dividing this total by 20. The maximum attainable score of 5 points indicates you believe using alcohol can be detrimental to your social, emotional, and physical well-being. A minimum score of 1 indicates you believe using alcohol can enhance your social, emotional, and physical well-being.

My Score is: _____ (Total Points)
                              20

SOURCE: Adapted from *Program Evaluation Handbook: Alcohol Abuse Education* (1988). Centers for Disease Control and the Office of Disease Prevention and Health Promotion, U.S. Department of Health and Human Services.

IDEAS ABOUT DRUG USE

This survey consists of 20 statements about how people might be affected by using illegal drugs. Read each statement, then put a checkmark in the column that best describes the way you feel about the statement.

		Strongly Agree	Agree	Not Sure	Disagree	Strongly Disagree
1.	Using drugs every day can lead to dependence on them.	( )	( )	( )	( )	( )
2.	Drug users usually have money problems.	( )	( )	( )	( )	( )
3.	People can use large amounts of marijuana without it hurting their families.	( )	( )	( )	( )	( )
4.	Cocaine users have more friends than other people.	( )	( )	( )	( )	( )
5.	People who regularly smoke marijuana don't really hurt anyone.	( )	( )	( )	( )	( )
6.	Using drugs causes people to lose self-control.	( )	( )	( )	( )	( )
7.	Regular marijuana users damage their health.	( )	( )	( )	( )	( )
8.	Using drugs makes people more creative.	( )	( )	( )	( )	( )
9.	Smoking marijuana is a good way to relax.	( )	( )	( )	( )	( )
10.	Using drugs helps people overcome boredom.	( )	( )	( )	( )	( )
11.	Cocaine improves one's ability to do one's job.	( )	( )	( )	( )	( )

	Strongly Agree	Agree	Not Sure	Disagree	Strongly Disagree
12. Regular drug users get into trouble with the law.	( )	( )	( )	( )	( )
13. Regular drug users have a hard time keeping friends.	( )	( )	( )	( )	( )
14. People who use sleeping pills rarely become dependent upon them.	( )	( )	( )	( )	( )
15. Using marijuana helps people understand themselves better.	( )	( )	( )	( )	( )
16. Heavy alcohol use hurts family relationships.	( )	( )	( )	( )	( )
17. Smoking cigarettes ages a person more quickly.	( )	( )	( )	( )	( )
18. People can stay perfectly healthy even if they regularly use illegal drugs.	( )	( )	( )	( )	( )
19. People who use illegal drugs have difficulty carrying out daily tasks.	( )	( )	( )	( )	( )
20. Smoking cigarettes helps control emotions like anger and frustration.	( )	( )	( )	( )	( )

SCORING AND ANALYSIS

Point values are assigned to responses as follows:

Item No.	Strongly Agree	Agree	Not Sure	Disagree	Strongly Disagree
1	5	4	3	2	1
2	5	4	3	2	1
3	1	2	3	4	5
4	1	2	3	4	5
5	1	2	3	4	5
6	5	4	3	2	1
7	5	4	3	2	1
8	1	2	3	4	5
9	1	2	3	4	5
10	1	2	3	4	5
11	1	2	3	4	5
12	5	4	3	2	1
13	5	4	3	2	1
14	1	2	3	4	5
15	1	2	3	4	5
16	5	4	3	2	1
17	5	4	3	2	1
18	1	2	3	4	5
19	5	4	3	2	1
20	1	2	3	4	5

This inventory should be scored by adding the point values of the responses from all questions. Divide this total by 20. The maximum attainable score of 5 points indicates you believe using illegal drugs is detrimental to your social, emotional, and physical well-being. A minimum score of 1 indicates you believe using illegal drugs can enhance your social, emotional, and physical well-being.

My Score is: _____ (Total Points)
                              20

SOURCE: Adapted from *Program Evaluation Handbook: Drug Abuse Education* (1988). Centers for Disease Control and the Office of Disease Prevention and Health Promotion, U.S. Department of Health and Human Services.

13

RISKY BUSINESS: HIGH-RISK/LOW-RISK ALCOHOL AND DRUG USE

In this exercise, you are asked to determine the level of risk you perceive to be present in the use of particular drugs. After you have designated a level of risk for each drug, you are asked to respond to several questions about how you determined the level of risk.

Examine the following list of drugs. Designate the level of risk involved in their use. In doing so, examine each drug as an individual entity; do not compare them.

1 = No Risk
2 = Low Risk
3 = Moderate Risk
4 = Significant Risk
5 = High Risk

_____ alcohol

_____ cocaine

_____ marijuana

_____ PCP

_____ valium

_____ speed

_____ crack

_____ acid (LSD)

_____ nicotine

_____ ludes (quaaludes)

_____ heroin

_____ mushrooms (psilocybin)

_____ codeine

_____ diet pills

1. How did you define risk?

2. What factors did you consider in that definition?

3. Which drugs entail the greatest risk for you personally?

4. How can you reduce the level of risk you take?

ATTITUDES TOWARD SMOKING

How do you feel about smoking? Circle the number in the column that most accurately describes how you feel about each of the following statements.

		Strongly Agree	Mildly Agree	Mildly Disagree	Strongly Disagree
1.	Cigarette smoking sets a bad example for children.	4	3	2	1
2.	Cigarette smoking is a messy and nasty habit.	4	3	2	1
3.	Smoking causes shortness of breath.	4	3	2	1
4.	Cigarettes cause damage to clothing and other personal items.	4	3	2	1
5.	Cigarette smoking causes serious health problems.	4	3	2	1
6.	Smoking is addictive.	4	3	2	1
7.	Quitting smoking helps a person live longer.	4	3	2	1
8.	Cigarette smoke is a significant health threat to nonsmokers.	4	3	2	1
9.	Nonsmokers rights should outweigh smokers rights.	4	3	2	1
10.	Cigarette smoking is unacceptable in public places.	4	3	2	1

SCORING AND ANALYSIS

Add up the points circled for each statement in order to determine your total score.

Total Score: _____

If your score is:

38-40	You are an anti-smoking radical! You have very negative attitudes toward smoking in general. You tend to believe that smoking is a health hazard, a bad habit, and is socially unacceptable.
31-37	Overall, you have a negative attitude toward smoking, but probably do not feel strongly enough to speak out on this issue.
20-30	You cannot make up your mind or you just do not care one way or the other. You do not understand why people make such a fuss about smoking.
15-19	You are probably a smoker who has good rationalization skills. Denial prevents many smokers from quitting.
10-14	Where have you been? You must be "out to lunch." Get educated about the realities of smoking!

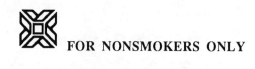 **FOR NONSMOKERS ONLY**

1. Have you ever smoked? If yes, when and why did you quit?

2. If you have never smoked, what made you decide not to try it?

3. How do you feel when others around you are smoking? How do you handle these situations?

4. Do you believe that smokers should be charged higher health insurance rates? Why or why not?

5. Do you believe that smoking should be prohibited in all public places? Why or why not?

 **HAVE A DRINK?**

> This survey describes various situations in which people often feel tempted to drink alcohol. Put a checkmark to show whether or not the situation leads you to want to have a drink.

	Definitely Yes	Probably Yes	Maybe	Probably No	Definitely No
1. You come home after a busy and frustrating day. You feel very tense and need to relax. Would this situation lead you to want a drink?	( )	( )	( )	( )	( )
2. It is Friday night and you have nothing to do. You have called several friends, but no one is home. Would this situation lead you to want to drink?	( )	( )	( )	( )	( )
3. You are at a party where everyone is drinking, dancing, and having a good time. Would this situation lead you to want to drink?	( )	( )	( )	( )	( )
4. You are feeling very anxious about a future event at school or work. You fear that it will not go well. Would this situation lead you to want to drink?	( )	( )	( )	( )	( )
5. You are at a party where you know very few people and you feel uncomfortable. Would this situation lead you to want to drink?	( )	( )	( )	( )	( )
6. You are spending a quiet evening at home. You have just found a good movie on television and have settled in to watch it. Would this situation lead you to want to drink?	( )	( )	( )	( )	( )

	Definitely Yes	Probably Yes	Maybe	Probably No	Definitely No
7. You are celebrating a special occasion at your favorite restaurant with friends. Would this situation lead you to want to drink?	( )	( )	( )	( )	( )
8. You are at a sporting event with some friends. Everyone is drinking beer and having fun. Would this situation lead you to want to drink?	( )	( )	( )	( )	( )
9. You have just had a disagreement with a family member. You are upset because the two of you seem to be having a difficult time getting along these days. Would this situation lead you to want a drink?	( )	( )	( )	( )	( )
10. You are at a holiday party given by the company you work for. There is an open bar and most of your co-workers are drinking. Would this situation lead you to want a drink?	( )	( )	( )	( )	( )

SCORING AND ANALYSIS

Point values are assigned to response options as follows:

Definitely Yes = 5
Probably Yes   = 4
Maybe   = 3
Probably No   = 2
Definitely No   = 1

This inventory should be scored by adding the point values of all your responses and dividing the total by 10. The maximum attainable score of 5 indicates you are strongly tempted to drink in a wide variety of situations. A score in the mid-range of 3 indicates that under some circumstances you may be tempted to drink. A low score around 1 indicates you are rarely tempted to drink, regardless of the situation.

My Score is:_____ (Total Points)
                10

Review your responses to the situations listed above and answer the following questions:

1. In what situations are you most tempted to drink alcohol and why?

2. In what situations are you least tempted to drink alcohol and why?

3. Some people tend to drink in response to unpleasant emotions, some in response to social pressures, and others as an antidote to boredom. Are there any patterns to your drinking behavior? If yes, what are they?

SOURCE: Adapted from *Program Evaluation Handbook: Alcohol Abuse Education* (1988). Centers for Disease Control and the Office of Disease Prevention and Health Promotion, U.S. Department of Health and Human Services.

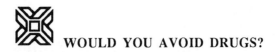

WOULD YOU AVOID DRUGS?

Below are 20 situations involving drugs. Read each situation, then put a checkmark in the column that best describes how confident you are that you would avoid using drugs in the situation described.

	Very Confident	Confident	Somewhat Confident	Not Very Confident	Not At All Confident
1. You have recently begun to go out with someone you like very much. One evening this person suggests that you smoke some crack. How confident are you that you would avoid smoking it?	( )	( )	( )	( )	( )
2. One weekend you get together with some friends. Soon, one friend begins passing around a bottle of whiskey. How confident are you that you would avoid drinking some?	( )	( )	( )	( )	( )
3. You are sitting with a group of your friends, and one lights up some marijuana to smoke. After a few people have smoked, the marijuana is passed to you. How confident are you that you would avoid smoking it?	( )	( )	( )	( )	( )
4. You successfully finish an important school project and decide to celebrate. One of your friends has LSD and says that tripping is a great way to party. How confident are you that you would avoid using it?	( )	( )	( )	( )	( )

	Very Confident	Confident	Somewhat Confident	Not Very Confident	Not At All Confident
5. A friend for whom you have a lot of respect suggests that you try marijuana and offers to smoke it with you. How confident are you that you would avoid smoking it?	( )	( )	( )	( )	( )
6. You are feeling very depressed about school. You remember that a friend gave you some amphetamines ("uppers," "speed"). How confident are you that you would avoid taking them?	( )	( )	( )	( )	( )
7. You must give a presentation in one of your classes. You are very nervous. Your best friend can get a mild tranquilizer (like Valium®) that would calm you down. How confident are you that you would avoid taking it?	( )	( )	( )	( )	( )
8. You are invited to a friend's house for the weekend. When you arrive, your friend offers you some mushrooms (psilocybin). How confident are you that you would avoid taking them?	( )	( )	( )	( )	( )
9. Several of your friends decide to smoke marijuana before an evening study session. They say that smoking marijuana will make studying easier. How confident are you that you would avoid smoking it?	( )	( )	( )	( )	( )
10. A friend of yours knows where to get "ecstacy" (MDMA) and offers to use it with you. You think of this friend as a trustworthy person. How confident are you that you would avoid using it?	( )	( )	( )	( )	( )

	Very Confident	Confident	Somewhat Confident	Not Very Confident	Not At All Confident
11. Your parents are out for the evening. Your cousin has some marijuana and offers to smoke it with you. You know that your parents won't be home for hours. How confident are you that you would avoid smoking it?	( )	( )	( )	( )	( )
12. You have sprained your ankle and are in pain. A friend has some prescription pain killers from a similar injury and offers them to you. How confident are you that you would avoid taking them?	( )	( )	( )	( )	( )
13. A friend who has begun to smoke marijuana seems to be developing a new set of friends and spending much less time with you. Someone suggests that if you smoked marijuana too, you might get to spend more time with your friend. How confident are you that you would avoid smoking it?	( )	( )	( )	( )	( )
14. You discover some Valium® (tranquilizers) in a drawer at home. No one is around and you are bored. How confident are you that you would avoid taking them?	( )	( )	( )	( )	( )
15. You feel pressured by the amount of homework you are being assigned. You wonder if having a couple of beers might relieve the pressure. How confident are you that you would avoid drinking them?	( )	( )	( )	( )	( )

	Very Confident	Confident	Somewhat Confident	Not Very Confident	Not At All Confident
16. During lunch, a friend introduces you to some people who are smoking cigarettes. Your friend decides to have a cigarette and offers you one. How confident are you that you would avoid smoking it?	( )	( )	( )	( )	( )
17. You go to a football game one weekend. One of your friends brings some vodka and passes it around. How confident are you that you would avoid drinking some?	( )	( )	( )	( )	( )
18. At a rock concert, the people next to you begin to use various drugs. They offer each drug to you. They are very nice to you and seem to be having a great time. How confident are you that you would avoid using the drugs?	( )	( )	( )	( )	( )
19. You are at a party, but you're feeling bored. Someone offers you some barbiturates ("downers," "reds"). How confident are you that you would avoid taking them?	( )	( )	( )	( )	( )
20. You go to a dance club. You meet some people from school who are going outside to use cocaine. They invite you along. How confident are you that you would avoid using it?	( )	( )	( )	( )	( )

SCORING AND ANALYSIS

Point values are assigned to responses as follows:

Very confident	=	5
Confident	=	4
Somewhat Confident	=	3
Not Very Confident	=	2
Not At All Confident	=	1

This inventory should be scored by adding the point values of all your responses and dividing the total by 20. The result is your average perceived ability to avoid drug use in general. The maximum attainable score of 5 points indicates a strong perceived ability to avoid using drugs. A minimum score of 1 indicates little or no perceived ability to avoid using drugs.

My Score is: _____ (Total Points)
                              20

Review your responses to the situations listed above and answer the following questions:

1. What factors influence your level of confidence in avoiding the use of drugs and why?

2. In what way does the type of drug (alcohol vs. marijuana vs. cocaine) influence your motivation and ability to avoid drug use?

3. In what way does the social situation influence your desire and ability to avoid drug use?

SOURCE: Adapted from *Program Evaluation Handbook: Drug Abuse Education* (1988). Centers for Disease Control and the Office of Disease Prevention and Health Promotion, U.S. Department of Health and Human Services.

REFRAINING FROM DRINKING

This survey describes situations when people often feel an urge to drink. Put a checkmark to show how sure you are that you could refrain from drinking in each situation if it were necessary.

Could you refrain from drinking if. . .	Definitely Yes	Probably Yes	Maybe	Probably No	Definitely No
1. you were eating an enjoyable meal?	( )	( )	( )	( )	( )
2. you were watching television?	( )	( )	( )	( )	( )
3. you were visiting friends, some of whom were drinking?	( )	( )	( )	( )	( )
4. you had just completed a difficult task that had taken you a long time to finish?	( )	( )	( )	( )	( )
5. you were tense and anxious?	( )	( )	( )	( )	( )
6. you had just had a big argument with someone in your family?	( )	( )	( )	( )	( )
7. you were relaxing after a busy day?	( )	( )	( )	( )	( )
8. you hadn't had a drink in a while and someone offered you one?	( )	( )	( )	( )	( )
9. you were waiting for a very important phone call that was fifteen minutes late?	( )	( )	( )	( )	( )
10. you were at a party and someone offered you a drink?	( )	( )	( )	( )	( )
11. you were at a sporting or entertainment event?	( )	( )	( )	( )	( )
12. you felt as if you really needed to drink?	( )	( )	( )	( )	( )
13. you were with a friend who urged you to drink?	( )	( )	( )	( )	( )

Could you refrain from drinking if. . .	Definitely Yes	Probably Yes	Maybe	Probably No	Definitely No
14. you were meeting a few friends in a bar or cocktail lounge?	( )	( )	( )	( )	( )
15. you were alone and feeling depressed?	( )	( )	( )	( )	( )
16. you were celebrating a special occasion?	( )	( )	( )	( )	( )
17. you were doing paperwork such as studying, paying bills, or writing a letter?	( )	( )	( )	( )	( )
18. you wanted to feel more sophisticated and attractive?	( )	( )	( )	( )	( )
19. you were bored?	( )	( )	( )	( )	( )
20. Could you refrain from drinking regardless of the circumstances?	( )	( )	( )	( )	( )

SCORING AND ANALYSIS

Point values are assigned to response options as follows:

Definitely Yes = 5
Probably Yes = 4
Maybe = 3
Probably No = 2
Definitely No = 1

This inventory should be scored by adding the point values of all your responses and dividing this total by 20. The maximum attainable score of 5 points indicates a strong perceived ability to refrain from drinking across a variety of potential drinking situations. A mid-range score of 3 indicates you are often unsure about your ability to refrain from drinking. A minimum score of 1 indicates a weak perceived ability to refrain from drinking in a variety of situations.

My Score is:_____ Total Points
                              20

Review your responses to the situations listed above and answer the following questions:

1. What factors influence your ability to refrain from drinking and why?

2. Under what circumstances are you most likely to drink and why?

3. Under what circumstances are you least likely to drink and why?

SOURCE: Adapted from *Program Evaluation Handbook: Alcohol Abuse Education* (1988). Centers for Disease Control and the Office of Disease Prevention and Health Promotion, U.S. Department of Health and Human Services.

 **DRUG DIARY**

For each day for two weeks, record every drug you take on the following forms. Include any prescription and over-the-counter drugs as well as alcohol, nicotine, caffeine, and street (illicit) drugs. Record the exact type and amount of the drug taken and the setting in which you took the drug. Also make note of your mood (angry, happy, depressed, bored, etc.) at the time you used the drug. Finally, make note of your stress level at the time, using the following level designations: 1. very relaxed, 2. low stress, 3. moderate stress, 4. very stressed. In order for this exercise to be a useful tool, you must be honest.

An example of a completed daily record follows:

DATE: *Friday, May 17, 1991*

	Type	Amount	Setting/mood	Stress
Prescription	*Birth Control Pill*	*1*	*home*	*1*
Over-the-counter	*Tylenol*	*2*	*school/headache*	*3*
Caffeine	*coffee*	*1 cup*	*home*	*2*
	pepsi	*16 oz.*	*school–lunch*	*2*
Nicotine	–			
Alcohol	*Beer*	*4*	*party*	*2*
Steroids	–			
Street drugs	–			

DATE:

	Type	Amount	Setting/mood	Stress
Prescription				
Over-the-counter				
Caffeine				
Nicotine				
Alcohol				
Steroids				
Street drugs				

DATE:

	Type	Amount	Setting/mood	Stress
Prescription				
Over-the-counter				
Caffeine				
Nicotine				
Alcohol				
Steroids				
Street drugs				

DATE:

	Type	Amount	Setting/mood	Stress
Prescription				
Over-the-counter				
Caffeine				
Nicotine				
Alcohol				
Steroids				
Street drugs				

DATE:

	Type	Amount	Setting/mood	Stress
Prescription				
Over-the-counter				
Caffeine				
Nicotine				
Alcohol				
Steroids				
Street drugs				

DATE:

	Type	Amount	Setting/mood	Stress
Prescription				
Over-the-counter				
Caffeine				
Nicotine				
Alcohol				
Steroids				
Street drugs				

DATE:

	Type	Amount	Setting/mood	Stress
Prescription				
Over-the-counter				
Caffeine				
Nicotine				
Alcohol				
Steroids				
Street drugs				

DATE:

	Type	Amount	Setting/mood	Stress
Prescription				
Over-the-counter				
Caffeine				
Nicotine				
Alcohol				
Steroids				
Street drugs				

DATE:

	Type	Amount	Setting/mood	Stress
Prescription				
Over-the-counter				
Caffeine				
Nicotine				
Alcohol				
Steroids				
Street drugs				

DATE:

	Type	Amount	Setting/mood	Stress
Prescription				
Over-the-counter				
Caffeine				
Nicotine				
Alcohol				
Steroids				
Street drugs				

DATE:

	Type	Amount	Setting/mood	Stress
Prescription				
Over-the-counter				
Caffeine				
Nicotine				
Alcohol				
Steroids				
Street drugs				

DATE:

	Type	Amount	Setting/mood	Stress
Prescription				
Over-the-counter				
Caffeine				
Nicotine				
Alcohol				
Steroids				
Street drugs				

DATE:

	Type	Amount	Setting/mood	Stress
Prescription				
Over-the-counter				
Caffeine				
Nicotine				
Alcohol				
Steroids				
Street drugs				

DATE:

	Type	Amount	Setting/mood	Stress
Prescription				
Over-the-counter				
Caffeine				
Nicotine				
Alcohol				
Steroids				
Street drugs				

DATE:

	Type	Amount	Setting/mood	Stress
Prescription				
Over-the-counter				
Caffeine				
Nicotine				
Alcohol				
Steroids				
Street drugs				

DRUG DIARY QUESTIONS

1. Did you notice any patterns in your use of drugs? If so, what patterns were evident?

2. Were you surprised about anything you noticed in your drug diary?

3. Are you concerned about your use of any specific drug or drugs? If so, what concerns you about it?

4. Do you consider your use of any particular drug to be excessive? If so, which one(s), and why do you think it is excessive?

5.　What, if any, effect did your mood have on your drug use?

6.　What, if any, effect did your stress level have on your drug use?

7.　Are any of your drug-taking behaviors in need of modification? If so, which ones?

8.　How might you modify these drug-taking behaviors?

LEVELS OF USE

> Read each statement carefully. If it is true for you, place a checkmark in the blank corresponding to that statement.

_____ you're young and feel strong

_____ use alcohol or drugs out of curiosity

_____ use them occasionally in social settings

_____ function well at school and home

Section A

_____ use alcohol or drugs for pleasure

_____ use drugs or drink regularly at social events

_____ using makes you feel like one of the group

_____ your rebellion is normal adolescent behavior

_____ behavior in school remains stable

Section B

_____ feel like you need to drink or use drugs

_____ feel in control

_____ use drugs or drink on a daily basis

_____ relationships with your family are becoming strained

_____ most of your friends do drugs or drink

_____ devote less time and attention to school work

_____ need to drink or use drugs to feel better

Section C

_____ have lost control over alcohol and drug use

_____ need to drink or use drugs to feel normal

_____ have had blackouts

_____ have not been taking care of your appearance, health

_____ may steal or commit other illegal acts

_____ tolerance to alcohol or specific drugs has increased

_____ use drugs or drink several times a day

Section D

_____ deny that you have a problem

_____ stop functioning completely at school, may even drop out

_____ become very depressed and even contemplate suicide

_____ may have withdrawal symptoms if you stop use of alcohol or drugs

_____ may blame others for your problems

Section E

SCORING AND ANALYSIS

Locate the section that has your last checkmark. If that √ falls in:

Section A:	You are an experimental user.
Section B:	You are a social/recreational user.
Section C:	You are in the beginning stages of abuse.
Section D:	You are in the advanced stages of abuse.
Section E:	You are addicted.

Now that you have completed the checklist, please answer the following questions:

1. Do you believe this is an accurate assessment of your use? If not, why not?

2. Is there anything about your use of alcohol or drugs that you want to change? If so, what is it, and how can you go about making the changes?

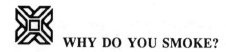

WHY DO YOU SMOKE?

This test is designed to provide you with a score on each of six factors that describe many people's feelings toward smoking. Three of these factors represent the *positive* feelings people get from smoking. The fourth is the *reduction of negative feelings,* such as a decrease in tension or anxiety. The fifth factor concerns a *craving* for smoking, which represents a dependence on cigarettes. The final factor is *habit* smoking, which takes place in an absence of feeling, or when smoking is purely automatic.

Circle the number that most accurately describes how you feel about each statement.

		Always	Fre-quently	Occa-sionally	Seldom	Never
A.	I smoke cigarettes to keep myself from slowing down.	5	4	3	2	1
B.	Handling a cigarette is part of the enjoyment of smoking it.	5	4	3	2	1
C.	Smoking cigarettes is pleasant and relaxing.	5	4	3	2	1
D.	I light up a cigarette when I feel angry about something.	5	4	3	2	1
E.	When I have run out of cigarettes I find it almost unbearable until I can get them.	5	4	3	2	1
F.	I smoke cigarettes automatically, without even being aware of it.	5	4	3	2	1
G.	I smoke cigarettes to stimulate me, to perk myself up.	5	4	3	2	1
H.	Part of the enjoyment of smoking a cigarette comes from the steps I take to light up.	5	4	3	2	1
I.	I find cigarettes pleasurable.	5	4	3	2	1
J.	When I feel uncomfortable or upset about something, I light up a cigarette.	5	4	3	2	1

		Fre- quently	Occa- sionally	Seldom	Never
	Always				
K. I am very much aware of the fact when I am not smoking a cigarette.	5	4	3	2	1
L. I light up a cigarette without realizing I still have one burning in the ashtray.	5	4	3	2	1
M. I smoke cigarettes to give me a "lift."	5	4	3	2	1
N. When I smoke a cigarette, part of the enjoyment is watching the smoke as I exhale it.	5	4	3	2	1
O. I want a cigarette most when I am comfortable and relaxed.	5	4	3	2	1
P. When I feel "blue" or want to take my mind off cares and worries, I smoke cigarettes.	5	4	3	2	1
Q. I get a real gnawing hunger for a cigarette when I haven't smoked for a while.	5	4	3	2	1
R. I've found a cigarette in my mouth and didn't remember putting it there.	5	4	3	2	1

SCORING AND ANALYSIS

Write the number you have circled after each statement in the corresponding space below.

Add the scores down each column to get your totals. For example, the sum of your scores for A, G, and M gives you the total score for the first column.

A ___	B ___	C ___	D ___	E ___	F ___
G ___	H ___	I ___	J ___	K ___	L ___
M ___	N ___	O ___	P ___	Q ___	R ___

Column Totals

1 ___	2 ___	3 ___	4 ___	5 ___	6 ___
Stimu- lation	Handling	Pleasure	Crutch	Craving	Habit

In this test, a score of 11 or above on any factor indicates that smoking is an important source of satisfaction for you. The higher your score (15 is the highest), the more important a particular factor is in your smoking and the more useful the discussion of that factor can be in your attempt to quit.

If you do not score high on any of the six factors, you, more than likely, do not smoke very much or have not been smoking for very many years. If so, giving up smoking—and staying off—should be easy.

The following categories describe motivations for smoking and suggest alternative activities to meet those needs.

1. Stimulation

If you score high or fairly high on this factor, you are one of those smokers who is stimulated by the cigarette—you feel that it helps to wake you up, organize your energies, and keep you going. If you try to give up smoking, you may want a safe substitute, such as a brisk walk or moderate exercise, whenever you feel the urge to smoke.

2. Handling

Handling things can be satisfying, but there are many ways to keep your hands busy without lighting up or playing with a cigarette. Why not toy with a pen or pencil? Or try doodling. Or play with a coin, a piece of jewelry, or some other harmless object.

3. Accentuation of Pleasure—Pleasurable Relaxation

It is not always easy to determine whether you use the cigarette to feel *good*, that is, get real, honest pleasure out of smoking (Factor 3), or to keep from feeling *bad* (Factor 4). About two-thirds of smokers score high or fairly high on *accentuation of pleasure,* and about half of those also score as high or higher on *reduction of negative feelings.*

Those who do get real pleasure out of smoking often find that honest consideration of the harmful effects of their habit is enough to help them quit. They substitute social and physical activities and find they do not seriously miss their cigarettes.

4. Reduction of Negative Feelings, or "Crutch"

Many smokers use cigarettes as a kind of crutch in moments of stress or discomfort. But the heavy smoker, the person who tries to handle severe personal problems by smoking many times a day, is apt to discover that cigarettes do not help in dealing with problems effectively.

When it comes to quitting, this kind of smoker may find it easy to stop when everything is going well, but may be tempted to start again in a time of crisis. Again, physical exertion or social activity may serve as useful substitutes for cigarettes, even in times of tension.

5. "Craving" or Dependence

Quitting smoking is difficult for the person who scores high on this factor. For the addicted smoker, the craving for a cigarette begins to build up the moment the cigarette is put out, so tapering off is not likely to work. This smoker must go "cold turkey."

If you are dependent on cigarettes, it may be helpful for you to smoke more than usual for a day or two, so that the taste for cigarettes is spoiled. Then isolate yourself completely from cigarettes until the craving is gone.

6. Habit

If you are smoking out of habit, you no longer get much satisfaction from your cigarettes. You just light them frequently without even realizing you are doing so. You may find it easy to quit and stay off if you can break the habit patterns you have created. Cutting down gradually may be quite effective if there is a change in the way the cigarettes are smoked and in the conditions under which they are smoked. The key to success is to become aware of each cigarette you smoke. This can be done by asking yourself, "Do I really want this cigarette?" You may be surprised at how many you do not want.

You must make two important decisions: 1) whether to go without the satisfactions you get from smoking or find an appropriate, less hazardous substitute activity, and 2) whether to cut out cigarettes all at once, or taper off. Your scores on this test should guide you in making these decisions.

ADDITIONAL RESOURCES

American Cancer Society*
777 Third Avenue
New York, NY 10017

American Heart Association*
7320 Greenville Avenue
Dallas, TX 75231

American Lung Association*
1740 Broadway
New York, NY 10019

Office of Cancer Communications
National Cancer Institute
National Institutes of Health
Bethesda, MD 20205

Office on Smoking and Health
5600 Fishers Lane
Room 1-10
Park Building
Rockville, MD 20857

---

*Consult your local telephone directory for listings of local chapters.

SOURCE: U.S. Department of Health and Human Services. 1983 Public Health Service. Publication No. (CDC) 75-8716

Our natural physical and psychological response to stress is referred to as strain. The 25 items below are examples of typical strain responses. That is, when we are experiencing stress, it is likely we will respond as described by one or more of the responses listed below.

This survey is designed to help you become more aware of your strain response patterns. It is not a complete list, by any means, but should provide a point of departure for further investigation.

Examine the following list of typical strain responses to stress. Then, according to how a particular response is true for you, assign a value to each item as follows:

0 = never

1 = infrequently

2 = frequently

3 = regularly

1. Eat too much
2. Drink too much alcohol
3. Smoke more than usual
4. Feel tense, uptight, fidgety
5. Feel depressed and remorseful
6. Like myself less
7. Have difficulty going to sleep or staying asleep
8. Feel restless and unable to concentrate
9. Have decreased interest in sex
10. Have increased interest in sex
11. Loss of appetite
12. Feel tired/low energy
13. Feel irritable

14. Think about suicide
15. Become less communicative
16. Feel disoriented or overwhelmed
17. Difficulty getting up in the morning
18. Headaches
19. Upset stomach
20. Sweaty and/or trembling hands
21. Underarm perspiration
22. Shortness of breath and sighing
23. Let things slide
24. Misdirected anger
25. Feel "unhealthy"

_____ TOTAL SCORE

SCORING AND ANALYSIS

Add the points from each item for your total score. If your score is over 30, you probably are experiencing high stress. It might be advisable for you to review the sources of stress in your life and attempt to remove some of them. You may also gain some insights from examining the pattern of your scores (e.g., circle all of your "3" responses and see if they are interrelated).

COPING STRATEGIES

Coping refers to how people respond when faced with stressful situations. By examining our coping behaviors, we can determine how we typically react to stressful situations and how appropriate and healthy our reactions are.

> Look at the following list of 40 responses, or coping behaviors, to stressful situations. If the behavior has been a typical reaction for you in a stressful situation, circle YES. If the behavior has not been typical of you, circle NO.

YES   NO   1.   Tried to relax or calm down by doing yoga, relaxation exercises, meditation, or other activities.

YES   NO   2.   Found or renewed faith.

YES   NO   3.   Engaged in an activity at home (e.g., craftwork, playing a musical instrument, painting), in a project at work, or in physical activity (e.g., sports, exercise, heavy work) in order to take my mind off the problem.

YES   NO   4.   Consulted a professional (doctor, psychologist, minister, etc.) for emotional support.

YES   NO   5.   Smoked more than usual.

YES   NO   6.   Resigned myself to the thought that life would be different because of the problem.

YES   NO   7.   Sought and received emotional comfort from members of my family.

YES   NO   8.   Tried to find some hope-sustaining beliefs.

YES   NO   9.   Calmed myself by eating some favorite food or by eating more than usual.

YES   NO   10.   Took action to prepare for dealing with the problem in the future.

YES   NO   11.   Calmed myself by drinking wine, beer, or spirits.

YES   NO   12.   Felt better after expressing anger toward the source of my problem or those responsible.

YES   NO   13.   Prayed and put my problem in God's hands.

YES   NO   14.   Worked to prevent the situation from getting worse by trying to anticipate what else could go wrong.

YES   NO   15.   Tried to take my mind off the problem by watching t.v., going to a movie, going shopping, or taking a trip, etc.

YES   NO   16.   Tried to view the problem as a challenge that I might get satisfaction in handling.

YES   NO   17.   Daydreamed or imagined a better time or place, or actively reminisced about times past.

YES   NO   18.   Read a book or magazine article looking for an answer, and searched for any new information that might be helpful.

YES   NO   19.   Relaxed myself by taking tranquilizers, marijuana, etc.

YES   NO   20.   Viewed the problem as less severe by realizing that there were many others in the same situation.

YES   NO   21.   Felt that only time would make a difference and nothing could be done, except wait.

YES   NO   22.   Made the situation seem more tolerable by realizing that things could be worse.

YES   NO   23.   Took out my frustrations on other people.

YES   NO   24.   Tried to get away from the problem for awhile by assuming extra responsibility at work.

YES   NO   25.   Prayed to God for support or strength to handle the problem myself.

YES   NO   26.   Sought and received emotional comfort from friends.

YES   NO   27.   Felt this was another of life's inevitable problems and chalked it up to fate or bad luck.

YES   NO   28.   Cried as a release.

YES   NO   29.   Tried to hang on until the problem resolved itself.

YES   NO   30.   Stayed close to home where I felt supported and needed.

YES   NO   31.   Complained about the problem, because I knew complaining would make me feel better.

YES   NO   32.   Tried to find the humorous aspects of the situation.

YES   NO   33.   Tried to develop alternative or possible solutions by negotiating with others.

YES   NO   34.   Generally adopted a more optimistic view of the problem.

YES   NO   35.   Accepted the hardship because it was meant to be.

YES   NO   36. Turned to my spiritual beliefs.

YES   NO   37. Thought over all the possible ways to solve the problem.

YES   NO   38. Did something reckless or unusual to get the frustration out of my system.

YES   NO   39. Talked to someone about how I was feeling.

YES   NO   40. Tried to get away from the problem for awhile by resting or sleeping more that usual.

SCORING AND ANALYSIS

Categories of coping responses:

Numbers	Type of Response
1, 5, 9, 11, 19	Relaxation — did something with the intent of relaxing (besides #1, a large number of "yes" answers to the other statements may point to problems with excessive use of alcohol and other drugs).
4, 7, 26, 30, 39	Social Support — sought or found emotional support from loved ones, friends or professionals.
2, 8, 13, 25, 36	Spiritual — sought or found spiritual comfort and support.
6, 21, 27, 29, 35	Resignation — accepted that the problem had occurred, but nothing could be done about it.
16, 20, 22, 32, 34	Cognitive reappraisal — tried to see the problem in a different light that made it seem more bearable.
10, 14, 18, 33, 37	Problem-solving strategies — thought about solutions to the problem, gathered information about it, or actually did something to try to solve it.
12, 23, 28, 31, 38	Self-expression — expressed emotions in response to the problem to reduce tension, anxiety, or frustration
3, 15, 17, 24, 40	Diversion — diverted attention away from the problem by thinking about other things or engaging in some activity.

If you circled yes to at least three items in any one category, this might indicate a pattern in your style of coping strategies. Think about which coping strategies are healthy and which ones are unhealthy, then decide if you may need to adapt or change your style of coping.

Healthy styles of coping:

Unhealthy styles of coping:

Styles I would like to adapt or change (if any):

SOURCE: Adapted from Stone and Neale. 1984. New measure of daily coping: Development and preliminary results. *Journal of Personality and Social Psychology.* V. 46 (4): 892-906.

ARE YOU A RISK TAKER?

Taking risks is sometimes scary and yet often necessary for emotional, intellectual, social, and physical development. Examine the following questions and respond as to whether or not you would take the risk.

		YES	NO
1.	Do you/would you ride a bicycle without a helmet?		
2.	Do you buckle your seat belt?		
3.	Would you go ocean kayaking?		
4.	Would you go rappelling on rock cliffs?		
5.	Would you cook and serve a new dish for company without testing it at another time?		
6.	If you wrote fiction or poetry, would you show it to others?		
7.	Would you say hello to a stranger on the street?		
8.	Would you go on a blind date?		
9.	Would you take friends to a new, exotic ethnic restaurant?		
10.	Would you play charades at a party?		
11.	Do you dive off the diving board at the pool?		
12.	Would you relocate to a distant city by yourself?		
13.	Would you go to a party when you know you will be a racial minority among invited guests?		
14.	Do you like to take risks?		
15.	Would you lend a friend your car to take on a long trip?		
16.	Would you tell someone that you like them very much, if you were uncertain of their reaction?		
17.	Would you ask a friend their honest opinion, even if it might hurt your feelings?		
18.	Do you answer questions in class even if you are unsure if they are correct?		
19.	Would you loan money to a friend if you were doubtful about their ability to repay you?		
20.	Would you challenge a professor who you believe is giving incorrect information in class?		

SCORING AND ANALYSIS

Risks can be classified into several categories.

Numbers	Type of Risk
5, 7, 8, 9, 10, 13	Social — are those you take in interpersonal relationships and/or in social situations for example, attending a party where you do not know anyone.
1, 2, 3, 4, 11	Physical — are those that expose you to possible bodily harm, like sky diving.
18, 20	Intellectual — are those that may reveal your lack of knowledge or inability to perform mental tasks.
6, 12, 16, 17	Emotional — are those that may expose you to emotional pain or hurt feelings.
15, 19	Financial — are those that expose you to possible monetary or property losses.

If you responded "yes" to two or more items in any one category, this might indicate a pattern in your risk-taking behavior. If you answered "yes" to two or more items in more than two categories you most likely are a person who enjoys taking a variety of risks.

1. What types of risks are you most likely to take and why?

2. What types of risks are you least likely to take and why?

LEISURE INTEREST CHECKLIST

For each activity listed, check (√) all columns which describe your level of interest in that particular activity.

ACTIVITY	LEVEL OF INTEREST IN THE PAST YEAR			Do you currently participate in this activity?		Do you ever use alcohol / drugs during this activity?		Would you like to pursue this in the future?	
	STRONG	SOME	NO	YES	NO	YES	NO	YES	NO
Gardening/Yardwork									
Sewing/Needlework									
Playing cards									
Church activities									
Walking									
Car repair									
Writing									
Dancing									
Golf									
Football									
Listening to music									
Holiday activities									
Movies									
Speeches/lectures									
Swimming									
Bowling									
Visiting friends									
Checkers/Chess									
Barbecues									
Reading									
Traveling									
Parties									
Wrestling									
Housecleaning									
Television									
Concerts									
Pottery									
Camping									
Laundry/Ironing									
Table games/pool									
Home decorating									
Clubs									
Singing									
Clothes									
Hairstyling									
Cycling									
Attending plays									
Bird watching									
Dating									
Auto-racing									

LEISURE INTEREST CHECKLIST

For each activity listed, check (√) all columns which describe your level of interest in that particular activity.

ACTIVITY	LEVEL OF INTEREST IN THE PAST YEAR			Do you currently participate in this activity?		Do you ever use alcohol / drugs during this activity?		Would you like to pursue this in the future?	
	STRONG	SOME	NO	YES	NO	YES	NO	YES	NO
Home repairs									
Exercise									
Hunting									
Woodworking									
Driving									
Child care									
Tennis									
Cooking/Baking									
Basketball									
Collecting									
Fishing									
Leatherwork									
Shopping									
Photography									
Painting/Drawing									

Totals

Count up the total for each of the following categories:

Total number of strong interests ...._____

Total number of activities in which you are currently participating.._____

Total number of activities during which you might use alcohol or other drugs ...._____

Total number of activities you would like to try in the future......_____

1. Compare the number of strong interests you have checked and the number of activities in which you currently participate. Is there a large or small gap between these two categories? What does this indicate?

2. Is there any pattern in your leisure interests? Do you tend to prefer physical, social, cultural, creative, or intellectual activities? Do you prefer group or solitary pursuits? Cooperative or competitive activities? Active or passive recreation?

3. To what extent are alcohol and other drugs associated with your leisure/recreational activities?

4. Choose one activity that you indicated an interest in trying in the future. Make the future today and get involved in this activity!

SOURCE: Adapted from Matsutsuyu. 1969. The interest checklist. *American Journal of Occupational Therapy*, 23: 323-328.

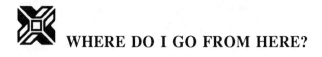

WHERE DO I GO FROM HERE?

After you have completed the self-assessments, you should have a clearer picture of where your strengths and weaknesses lie.

Do you have adequate information

on which to base your decisions regarding drug and alcohol use?

How do your attitudes contribute to your decisions

to use or not to use alcohol and other drugs?

Is your behavior consistent with your knowledge and attitudes

about drug and alcohol use?

The following skill-building section assists you in developing the thought processes and skills necessary to achieve a healthy perspective on drug and alcohol use. Some of the skills addressed include decision making, self-monitoring, coping with stressful situations, assertiveness, and determining your blood alcohol concentration. In addition, this section seeks to help you identify healthy, drug-free recreational alternatives.

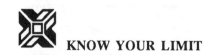 **KNOW YOUR LIMIT**

Drinking and driving is a very serious problem in the United States. It is estimated that between 40 and 50 percent of all traffic fatalities are alcohol-related. In addition, alcohol-related automobile crashes are the leading cause of death for young people between the ages of 16 and 24. Obviously, high-school and college-age students are particularly vulnerable.

How can you tell if you have had too much to drink and should not drive? The following simple formula can give you an <u>estimate</u> of your blood alcohol concentration (BAC). Remember this is only an estimate.

$$\frac{\text{\# of drinks - \# of hours x weight factor}}{100} = \text{BAC}$$

<u>Steps in the Calculation:</u>

1. Count the number of drinks you have had, and subtract the number of hours you have been drinking.

2. Multiply the figure calculated in step 1 by the weight factor. If you are 150 pounds or less, the weight factor is 3. If you are over 150 pounds, the weight factor is 2.

3. Divide this product by 100 to determine your BAC.

In most states, the BAC that constitutes Driving While Intoxicated (DWI) is .10, but some states are in the process of lowering the legal limit to .07 or .08.

If your estimated BAC is .10 or greater, you <u>must</u> <u>not</u> drive. Call a cab, call your parents, or ask a friend to drive you home. It is always best never to drink to the point of intoxication, but if you do, "designate a driver."

Often, when we are drinking, we believe we are functioning normally and are perfectly capable of driving. More often than not, this is untrue because on a physiological level, alcohol impairs our judgment. Know your limit ahead of time and stick to it!

QUESTIONS

1. If you were at a party for three hours and drank six beers, what would your BAC be?

2. If you were out with a friend and you noticed that he drank five beers and three mixed drinks during the course of a three hour period, would you let him drive home? Why or why not?

3. If you drink, think of a typical situation in which you are drinking. Calculate your BAC based on your usual drinking pattern.

   If you do not drink, ask a friend to tell you about the average number of drinks they would have in a party situation and calculate their BAC.

RESPONSIBLE VS. IRRESPONSIBLE ALCOHOL USE

> The prevailing societal attitude regarding alcohol consumption is that people should use alcohol responsibly. Yet, how do we define responsible drinking? Indicate whether you consider the following examples responsible or irresponsible and then <u>describe your reasons for reaching this conclusion.</u>

1. Janet is at her neighbor's party. She has been on prescribed medication for ten days but isn't sure if it reacts with alcohol—there was no warning on her prescription. She gets thirsty and drinks a couple of beers, since it is the only beverage available.

2. Ed's girlfriend and family expressed concern over his drinking on Friday and Saturday nights (about eight beers each night). Ed feels he's fine because, after all, "I only drink on weekends, otherwise I'm in control."

3. Four teenagers go swimming together at a nearby pond a half-dozen times over the course of a summer. Each time they take along a case of beer.

4. Mr. and Mrs. Roberts like to drink wine with dinner. They give a little bit to their five-year-old son and eight-year-old daughter.

5. The DMZ fraternity house holds a Saturday night beer blast. Females are allowed to drink as much beer as they want for free. Males are charged 50 cents for each beer.

6. Adam, David, and Joe are 19-year-old sophomores at the University of Maryland. Each of them sneaks one "airline miniature" bottle of rum into Byrd Stadium for a football game. They pour the rum into a soda that they buy.

7. Bill plans on getting drunk at a local bar on Friday night and asks a friend to be a designated driver. On Friday the friend does not show up, so Bill drives home drunk.

8. Betsy finally had enough nerve to arrange a date with Tim. Tim suggested they have some drinks and bought two rounds of Mai-Tais. Betsy went ahead and drank them so she wouldn't offend Tim, even though she could take or leave alcohol.

DECIDING ABOUT DRUG USE

List a drug you use now or are thinking about using. Write out arguments for and against the use of this drug. Some of these arguments may be personal, and others, scientific in nature. Write your decision at the bottom of the page. Remember alcohol, nicotine, caffeine, and even the birth control pill are drugs which require you to use a decision-making process.

DRUG:

For (positive effects)

1. Effects on the body

2. Effects on the mind

3. Effect on values

4. Legality

Against (negative effects)

Effects on the body

Effects on the mind

Effect on values

Legality

5. Effect on your human potential   Effect on your human potential

6. Effect on family   Effect on family

7. Other effects   Other effects

RESOLUTION: Write down your decision. Will this decision change as you age? As your
                         social situation changes?

 **DRAW THE LINE**

As much as we would like, the decision whether or not to use drugs is not always clear-cut. There are ambiguities when trying to classify drug use, misuse, and abuse.

In certain circumstances, the use of drugs is accepted and even condoned (i.e., taking antibiotics to cure disease, taking Valium® to relieve anxiety). However, in other circumstances, the use of drugs is highly frowned upon (i.e., drinking alcohol then driving an automobile). Have you ever wondered why this is? It is usually an individual decision as to what substances or drugs a person feels are acceptable in a situation.

When making these decisions, we are making judgments depending on our values. Values can be shaped by attitudes, beliefs, education, family, and friends. In the following situations, check whether you feel the use of drugs would be acceptable or unacceptable.

		Acceptable	Un-acceptable
1.	Taking cough syrup with codeine for a bad cough.	_____	_____
2.	Taking heroin for pain relief in the case of a cancer patient.	_____	_____
3.	Smoking marijuana for better sight in the case of a person with glaucoma.	_____	_____
4.	Drinking coffee to help you get through the day.	_____	_____
5.	Snorting cocaine/smoking crack to help you get through the day.	_____	_____
6.	Drinking coffee to help someone stay up to study for a big exam/finish a big project.	_____	_____
7.	Taking amphetamines to help someone stay up to study for a big exam/finish a big project.	_____	_____
8.	Taking some pills or drinking to help ease the pain of the death of a friend/parent/spouse/child.	_____	_____
9.	Having a drink to relax after a long day at work/school.	_____	_____

	Acceptable	Un-acceptable

10. Taking some type of drug to avoid thinking about a bad home situation (parents always fighting, getting abused). _____ _____

11. Drinking alcohol to avoid boredom. _____ _____

12. Drinking alcohol at meals. _____ _____

13. Drinking alcohol with friends at a party. _____ _____

14. Smoking marijuana with friends at a party. _____ _____

15. Having a cigarette to start your day/after a meal. _____ _____

16. Parents smoking cigarettes in front of children. _____ _____

17. Parents smoking marijuana in front of children. _____ _____

18. Taking aspirin for a headache. _____ _____

19. Taking your parent's or a friend's pain medication for a bad headache or other body aches. _____ _____

20. Using diet pills to lose weight. _____ _____

21. Using something to forget about a bad experience (bad grades, breakup with boyfriend/girlfriend). _____ _____

22. Talking to a friend about his/her drug use. _____ _____

23. Talking to a parent about his/her drug use. _____ _____

24. Smoking when pregnant. _____ _____

25. Drinking small amounts of alcohol when pregnant. _____ _____

26. Taking a drink when offered by a parent. _____ _____

27. Drinking alcohol at home from parents' supply. _____ _____

28. Taking a higher dose than recommended to get rid of bad feelings quicker (an extra tablespoon of Nyquil®, three aspirin instead of two, two Valium® for an extra stressful day). _____ _____

QUESTIONS

1. Were there any patterns to your responses?

2. Was there consistency in your responses (i.e., not okay to smoke cigarettes or marijuana in front of children)?

3. What is there about smoking both marijuana and cigarettes in front of children that is not consistent?

4. What factors influence your decision making when deciding whether or not to use drugs?

5. How do you personally decide whether a situation is drug use, misuse, or abuse?

 CHOICES

Many individuals detest the use of medication. Yet, in the case of pain, certain drugs can be very effective. Perhaps a person's resistance to pain-killing drugs is dictated by the situation. In the following scenarios, indicate whether you would resist pain-killing drugs, prefer pain-killing drugs, or definitely want such drugs. Remember the term pain-killing drugs includes such common household drugs as aspirin and Tylenol®.

Event	No drugs	Perhaps	Definitely	Why/why not?
Having a dental cavity filled				
Recovering from a broken leg				
Experiencing a migraine headache				
Recovering from a severely sprained wrist				
Delivering a baby				
Severe intestinal cramps and diarrhea				
Dying of cancer				
Lacerations from a car accident which require stitches				

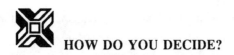

HOW DO YOU DECIDE?

This test presents descriptions of people who are trying to make decisions that may affect their health or the health of others. Read each item. Then answer the follow-up question by circling the letter of the **next** step that the person should take in order to make a decision using a systematic approach.

This test measures your ability to identify the steps in a systematic decision-making process.

This exercise assumes decision making to be a systematic process involving five steps:

1. identifying/clarifying the decision to be made,
2. identifying possible decision options,
3. gathering/processing information,
4. making/implementing the decision, and
5. evaluating the decision.

1. Cindy has been invited to a party where other people will probably be smoking marijuana. Cindy has never smoked marijuana, but she is curious about it. She wants to decide what to do if someone at the party offers her marijuana. Cindy thinks about what she might do. She also thinks what her best friend would do. Cindy goes to the library and reads some books on marijuana. She decides not to smoke at the party. While at the party, Cindy is offered marijuana several times but turns down the offers.

    What is the best thing for Cindy to do **next** in order to use the systematic decision-making approach?

    A. Ask her friends if they have ever smoked marijuana.
    B. Think about whether she's happy about her decision.
    C. Avoid the people who offered her marijuana at the party.
    D. Read more books about marijuana.

2. Terri has not been feeling well for the past few months. She went to her doctor for some tests and was informed that she has cancer. She is frightened that she will become a terrible burden for her family and, eventually, die of her illness. However, Terri knows that she must make a decision about what she is going to do. After talking with several doctors, she learned that she has several options. She could enter an experimental drug treatment program, or she could just wait to see if her health improves. She talks to her husband about her feelings and fears.

What is the best thing for Terri to do **next** in order to use the systematic decision-making approach?

   A. Decide to wait and see if her illness gets better on its own.
   B. Get more information about each of her treatment options.
   C. Go to another doctor to get a different opinion.
   D. Go on a vacation with her family to help her forget about her problem.

3. Todd drinks every day and he often drinks by himself. He frequently can't remember things that happened after drinking. Todd has tried to quit drinking many times but has been unsuccessful. Todd is afraid he might lose his job if anyone finds out about his drinking.

What is the best thing for Todd to do **next** in order to use the systematic decision-making approach?

   A. Take a week off from work and try to stop drinking on his own.
   B. Ask his doctor to select a drinking program for him to attend.
   C. Read some articles about drinking and its effects on health.
   D. Realize that he must decide what kind of help to get to reduce his drinking.

4. David has made some big changes in his life. He moved and will also be starting a new school in a few weeks. He is very nervous about school. David recognizes that all these changes may cause stress. He also knows there are ways to reduce it. He wants to choose a way to reduce some of the stress he's feeling.

   What is the best thing for David to do **next** in order to use the systematic decision-making approach?

   A. Start a regular exercise program.
   B. Think about the things he likes to do that seem to relax him.
   C. Decide on a way to relieve the stress he feels.
   D. Ask his family to choose a way for him to reduce stress.

5. Shelley recently moved into the dormitory for her first year of college. The students on her floor share a kitchen. Shelley soon finds that she is eating a great deal of quick, high-calorie snacks. She is gaining weight and doesn't feel as energetic as usual. She realizes that she needs to decide on a plan for eating more healthy meals.

   What is the best thing for Shelley to do **next** in order to use the systematic decision-making approach?

   A. Find out how much it would cost to eat in the university cafeteria.
   B. Think of the possible options that are available to her.
   C. Realize she needs to start eating balanced meals.
   D. Ask her mother to decide what she should do.

6. Joyce wants to stop smoking. She knows there are many ways to quit and that she should choose the best way for her. She discusses the matter with a friend. They come up with several plans. Joyce could stop smoking completely on a certain day, or she could smoke a little less every day until she stops completely. She thinks about which approach would be easiest for her and talks to other people who have already quit smoking.

   Joyce decides to stop smoking gradually. At the start of every week she reduces the number of daily cigarettes she smokes by three. Unfortunately, Joyce isn't too happy with her new plan because she has trouble keeping track of the number of cigarettes she smokes.

What is the best thing for Joyce to do **next** in order to use the systematic decision-making approach?

A. Call up some stop-smoking clinics to find out about approaches they use.
B. Think again about her decision to stop smoking.
C. Stick with her decision for at least a month regardless of how she feels about it.
D. Give up on the gradual approach and stop smoking completely on a particular day.

SCORING AND ANALYSIS

Correct answers:

1.	B		4.	B
2.	B		5.	B
3.	D		6.	B

Count up your correct answers, and find out how you rate:

6	Excellent
5	Good
4	Fair
3 or less	You may need some help in developing systematic decision-making skills.

SOURCE: Adapted from *Program Evaluation Handbook: Alcohol Abuse Education* (1988). Centers for Disease Control and the Office of Disease Prevention and Health Promotion, U.S. Department of Health and Human Services.

WHAT CAUSES YOU STRESS?

Hans Selye, a renowned stress researcher, defined stress as the nonspecific response of the body to any demand made upon it. A stressor, which is an event that triggers the physiological stress response, can be negative (i.e., a traffic ticket or an exam) or positive (i.e., a first date with someone you really like). Typically, the negative stressors are the ones that cause us distress.

The following exercise is aimed at assisting you in identifying stressors in different areas of your life and examining how you cope with those stressors. Be as specific and concrete as you can.

1. Identify two academic or class stressors (i.e., the required use of a computer in a class). Be as specific and concrete as possible in your description of the stressors.

How do you currently cope with each of these stressors?

Give some thought as to how you could handle each stressor differently. Develop a specific plan for altering your response. Explain your plan in detail.

2.   Identify two stressors in your personal life, such as in relationships with friends/family, career issues, residence hall living, etc. Be as specific and concrete as possible in your description of the stressors.

How do you currently cope with each of these stressors?

Give some thought as to how you could handle each stressor differently. Develop a specific plan for altering your response. Explain your plan in detail.

3.   Identify one physical symptom of stress that you experience often. Be as specific and concrete as possible in your description of the stressors.

How do you currently cope with each of these stressors?

Give some thought as to how you could handle each stressor differently. Develop a specific plan for altering your response. Explain your plan in detail.

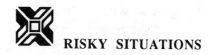 RISKY SITUATIONS

Examine the following list of situations. Designate the level of risk you perceive to be present in each. In doing so, examine each scenario as an individual entity and do not compare them. After you have designated a level of risk for each scenario, respond to the questions on the following page as to how you determined that level of risk.

1 = No Risk
2 = Low Risk
3 = Moderate Risk
4 = Significant Risk
5 = High Risk

_____ going home with someone you just met in a bar

_____ smoking marijuana in the residence hall

_____ riding home in a car with someone who has been drinking

_____ trying crack for the first time

_____ combining drinking and drug use

_____ going to a frat party

_____ partying during spring break

_____ drinking the night before an exam

_____ smoking a pack of cigarettes a day

_____ having sex after drinking or using drugs

_____ using a false ID to buy alcohol

_____ driving a car after smoking marijuana

_____ taking an exam while "high"

_____ buying drugs from someone you do not know

QUESTIONS

1. How did you define risk?

2. Are there different types of risk?

3. What factors did you consider in that definition?

4. In which scenario would you be more likely to take a significant or high risk ?

5. How can you reduce your level of risk?

 **ALTERNATIVES**

Below is a list of reasons given by people for using drugs and alcohol. Read each motive, then write several possible alternatives to drug and alcohol use.

MOTIVE FOR DRUG/ALCOHOL USE	POSSIBLE ALTERNATIVES
Example: Need for relaxation	Playing music; walking; meditation
To escape boredom	
Peer pressure	
To feel "high"	
Depression	
To feel less inhibited	
Kicks, risks, trying something new	

 **DRUG-FREE HIGHS**

The desire to experience euphoria or an altered state of consciousness is as natural as sleep according to some experts. The perception of euphoria is influenced by a number of factors and varies from individual to individual.

In the space provided, indicate the benefits and the disadvantages to drug-induced euphoria and natural euphoria.

Drug-induced Euphoria

Benefits	Disadvantages
1.	
2.	
3.	

Natural Euphoria

Benefits	Disadvantages
1.	
2.	
3.	

Altered states of consciousness are characterized by a focus on the here and now, a loss of immediate memory, and a transcendence of one's personal boundaries. It is a receptive, sensation-oriented, feeling state. Altered states of consciousness can be induced by bombarding the senses, depriving the senses, or presenting the senses with constant repetition.

Typically, activities that produce an altered state of consciousness usually involve one or more of the following:

A. an element of risk, such as skydiving
B. multi-sensory, such as a rock concert
C. timelessness/spacelessness, such as meditation
D. loss of self/ego boundaries, such as a group hug or some spiritual experiences
E. strong emotion, such as fear or love
F. constant rhythm and repetition, such as running

Based on the above descriptions, list ten drug-free activities that have the potential for inducing euphoria and/or an altered state of consciousness.

1.

2.

3.

4.

5.

6.

7.

8.

9.

10.

DO OTHERS INFLUENCE YOUR DECISIONS? ARE YOU AN INDEPENDENT THINKER?

Most of us are influenced by others when making decisions for ourselves, which is only natural. During the adolescent and young adult years, the influences of others may be especially important. We want to impress friends, yet at the same time we may experience conflict with friends and parents when trying to formulate our own ideas.

The "family and friends" sections will help you determine those who are your primary influences. The exercises in these sections are designed to examine how susceptible you are to peer pressure and how assertive you are should you need to resist that peer pressure.

Characteristics of family members within dysfunctional families will also be examined. The term "dysfunctional family" refers to a family in which someone has a problem with alcohol or some other type of drug. Other factors contribute to dysfunctional families as well.

Finally, there are some exercises, using role-playing and intervention scenarios, that give you a chance to think about what you would do if confronted with a situation where you needed to talk to a friend or family member regarding their use of alcohol or other drugs.

RECOGNIZING THE ROLE OF ALCOHOL AND OTHER DRUGS IN OUR RELATIONSHIPS

The use of alcohol and drugs can have a profound impact on our relationships today and in the future. Many of us struggle with being assertive or handling problems with friends that occur even as a routine part of life. Using alcohol and drugs can pose further challenges for relationships between friends, and having a friend develop a problem with alcohol or drugs can be a difficult and trying experience. For those who grew up in homes where alcohol or drug abuse may have been a problem for a parent, awareness of its influence on one's behaviors, self image, and relationships can be very useful.

In this section, you will have the opportunity to explore the role of alcohol and drugs in your relationships with friends and family members. By doing these exercises, you will be able to: (1) recognize how alcohol and drug use, and your beliefs about their use, may have affected you and your relationships, (2) examine your behavior in various situations with friends and family, and (3) assess whether a friend or family member is in trouble with alcohol and drugs. The knowledge you gain through these exercises can provide the basis for changing your behavior and improving your relationships.

 **FRIENDS**

This survey deals with how your friends feel about drug use. Read each statement carefully, then put a checkmark in the most appropriate column.

		All of My Friends	Most of My Friends	Some of My Friends	A Few of My Friends	None of My Friends
1.	How many of your friends would be upset if you took them to a party where drugs were being used?	( )	( )	( )	( )	( )
2.	How many of your friends would think that it was all right for you to use diet pills if you wanted to lose weight?	( )	( )	( )	( )	( )
3.	How many of your friends would be angry if you used marijuana, even if it was the first time you'd tried it?	( )	( )	( )	( )	( )
4.	How many of your friends would be upset if you tried cocaine ("coke," or "crack") just once, to see what it is like?	( )	( )	( )	( )	( )
5.	How many of your friends would disapprove of you having other friends who occasionally use drugs?	( )	( )	( )	( )	( )
6.	How many of your friends would understand if you took a tranquilizer (like Valium®) because you were very nervous about a test?	( )	( )	( )	( )	( )
7.	How many of your friends would be upset if you rode in a car driven by someone who had been drinking alcohol?	( )	( )	( )	( )	( )
8.	How many of your friends would be angry if you got drunk on an important occasion, like a graduation party or New Year's Eve?	( )	( )	( )	( )	( )

	All of My Friends	Most of My Friends	Some of My Friends	A Few of My Friends	None of My Friends
9. How many of your friends consider it normal for students to experiment with drugs?	( )	( )	( )	( )	( )
10. How many of your friends would take LSD ("acid") with you, if you asked them?	( )	( )	( )	( )	( )

SCORING AND ANALYSIS

Point values are assigned to responses as follows:

Item Number	All of My Friends	Most of My Friends	Some of My Friends	A Few of My Friends	None of My Friends
1	5	4	3	2	1
2	1	2	3	4	5
3	5	4	3	2	1
4	5	4	3	2	1
5	5	4	3	2	1
6	1	2	3	4	5
7	5	4	3	2	1
8	5	4	3	2	1
9	1	2	3	4	5
10	1	2	3	4	5

This inventory should be scored by adding the point values of all your responses and dividing the total by 10. The maximum attainable score of 5 points indicates you perceive your friends to be opposed to illegal or irresponsible drug use. A mid-range score of 3 indicates you have some friends who are opposed to drug use and some who accept it. A minimum score of 1 suggests you perceive your friends to be accepting or encouraging of illegal or irresponsible drug use.

My Score is:_____ (Total Points)
                              10

Based on your perceptions of your friends' attitudes toward drug use, answer the following questions:

1. How do your friends' attitudes toward drug use influence your behavior?

2. Do you and your friends have similar attitudes toward drug use? In what ways are they similar, and in what ways do they differ?

3. Do you ever feel unwanted peer pressure from your friends regarding alcohol or drug use? How do you typically handle these situations?

4. Peer pressure is not always negative. Give two examples of "positive" peer pressure.

 **CIRCLE OF FRIENDS**

Friends affect our behavior in a variety of subtle and obvious ways. This exercise is designed to examine their influence on your alcohol and drug use.

Directions:

1.   Write your name in the center circle.

2.   In circle A, write the names of the friends who are closest to you, those with whom you share the strongest relationships, and those friends who are the most important in your life.

3.   In circle B, write the names of the friends who are important to you but are not as close to you as those friends listed in circle A.

4.   In circle C, write the names of casual friends, those with whom you interact but who are not as important in your life as those listed in the other circles.

5.   Now review those names and place a star/asterisk next to the names of those friends who use drugs (including alcohol and tobacco).

6.   How do these friends influence your use of drugs (including alcohol and tobacco)?

Circle of Friends

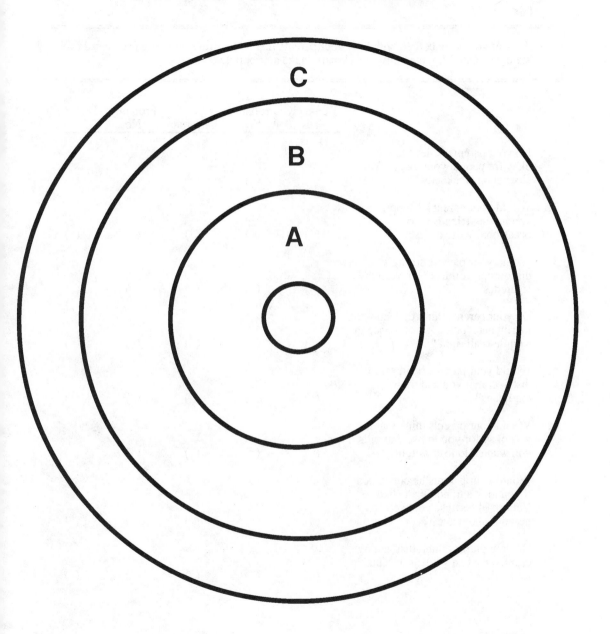

WHAT DO MY PARENTS THINK?

> This survey is concerned with how your parents feel about drugs and drug use. Read each statement carefully, then put a checkmark in the appropriate column.

		Definitely Yes	Probably Yes	Uncertain	Probably No	Definitely No
1.	Do your parents believe that it is okay for people your age to drink alcohol on weekends?	( )	( )	( )	( )	( )
2.	Would your parents disapprove of you having friends who occasionally use drugs?	( )	( )	( )	( )	( )
3.	Would your parents strongly discourage you from smoking cigarettes?	( )	( )	( )	( )	( )
4.	Do your parents think that smoking marijuana ("pot," "grass") once in a while is all right?	( )	( )	( )	( )	( )
5.	Would your parents be upset to discover that you had tried marijuana?	( )	( )	( )	( )	( )
6.	Would your parents think that it was okay for you to use diet pills if you wanted to lose weight?	( )	( )	( )	( )	( )
7.	Would your parents be concerned if you took a tranquilizer (like Valium®) because you were very nervous about a test?	( )	( )	( )	( )	( )
8.	Do your parents think that getting drunk once in a while is acceptable for adults?	( )	( )	( )	( )	( )

	Definitely Yes	Probably Yes	Uncertain	Probably No	Definitely No
9. Would your parents be upset if you rode in a car driven by someone who had been drinking alcohol?	( )	( )	( )	( )	( )
10. Would your parents be upset if you got drunk on a special occasion, like graduation day or New Year's Eve?	( )	( )	( )	( )	( )

SCORING AND ANALYSIS

Point values are assigned to responses as follows:

Item Number	Definitely Yes	Probably Yes	Uncertain	Probably No	Definitely No
1	1	2	3	4	5
2	5	4	3	2	1
3	5	4	3	2	1
4	1	2	3	4	5
5	5	4	3	2	1
6	1	2	3	4	5
7	5	4	3	2	1
8	1	2	3	4	5
9	5	4	3	2	1
10	5	4	3	2	1

This inventory should be scored by adding the point values of all your responses and dividing the total by 10. The maximum attainable score of 5 points indicates you perceive your parents to be opposed to illegal or irresponsible drug use. A mid-range score of 3 indicates you perceive your parents to be inconsistent or uncertain about their attitudes towards alcohol or drug use. A minimum score of 1 suggests you perceive your parents to be accepting of illegal or irresponsible drug use.

Review your responses to the survey and answer the following questions:

1. Do you notice any inconsistencies in your parents' attitudes toward alcohol and drug use? If yes, please describe.

2. Are your attitudes toward alcohol and drug use similar or dissimilar to your parents'? In what way?

3. In what ways do your parents' attitudes toward alcohol and drug use affect your behavior?

HOW ASSERTIVE ARE YOU?

The items below represent situations in which one can behave in an assertive or non-assertive manner. Place a checkmark in the column which you feel is most appropriate. Answer the questions as honestly as you can in order to learn from your test.

	Always	Usually	Some-times	Seldom	Never
1. Do you suppress what you feel?					
2. Do you keep your opinions to yourself?					
3. Do you find it difficult to begin a conversation with a stranger?					
4. Do you find it difficult to express love and affection?					
5. Is it difficult for you to compliment and praise others?					
6. Do you admire people who "turn the other cheek"?					
7. Do "bossy" people intimidate you?					
8. If a salesman has gone to considerable trouble to show you some merchandise which is not quite suitable, do you have difficulty in saying "no"?					
9. If you objected, how likely would you be to confront a roommate using drugs in your room?					
10. Do you keep quiet "for the sake of peace"?					
11. Would you drive a few extra miles rather than ask a stranger for directions?					
12. Do you make no protest when someone cuts in front of you in a line?					
13. If your friend wanted to drive home despite his/her drunkenness, would you confront and/or take action to stop him/her?					
14. Do you complain to others rather than those who offend you?					
15. Would you be very reluctant to return a garment bought a few days previously and which you discover to be faulty?					
16. Do you find it difficult to contradict a domineering person?					

	Always	Usually	Some-times	Seldom	Never
17. If someone stole your parking space would you merely drive on?					
18. If food that is not to your satisfaction is served at a restaurant, would you eat it without complaint?					
19. Are you careful to avoid hurting the feelings of others?					
20. If a friend makes what you consider to be an unreasonable request, do you comply rather than take a stand?					

SCORING AND ANALYSIS

If you have responded on the majority of items with "always" and "usually," you may not be acting as assertively as you potentially can. However, for items 9 and 13, an "always" or "usually" response indicates assertive behavior.

Now, examine your responses for each item and answer the following questions :

1. In what situations and with which people are you most likely to be assertive? Why?

2. In what situations and with which people are you least likely to be assertive? Why?

3. What are the obstacles to your assertive behavior in the situations you listed?

4. What kinds of changes can you make in order to be more assertive in these situations?

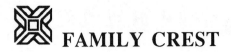 **FAMILY CREST**

Our families have a profound impact on who we are and how we behave. This exercise examines your relationships within your family and helps you describe your family's characteristics, strengths, and weaknesses.

<u>Directions:</u>

1.   In box A, write your name and the three personality characteristics that are your greatest assets.

2.   In box B, draw a symbol or picture that characterizes your relationship with your family.

3.   In box C, draw your nuclear family, using Xs for males and Os for females, labeling each with the names of family members.

4.   In box D, write the name of the person in your family with whom you feel the closest emotional bond. List three personality characteristics that you admire in this person.

5.   In box E, write the name of the person in your family with whom you feel the most emotional distance and in a few words, describe why you feel this way.

6.   In box F, list five characteristics which describe your family as a whole.

When you have completed the Family Crest, answer the following questions.

1.   What do you believe are your family's strengths?

2.   What are your family's weaknesses?

FAMILY CREST

A

B

C

D

E

F

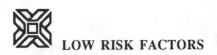 **LOW RISK FACTORS**

> The National Institute on Alcohol Abuse and Alcoholism summarized the existing literature and found the following factors were indicative of adults who have the fewest problems with alcohol. Which of these factors apply to you? Check the items that apply to you.

_____ 1. You were exposed to alcohol in relatively small quantities early in life by your family or within the context of a religious or cultural group.

_____ 2. Your family members viewed alcohol as a food and consumed small quantities primarily at mealtime.

_____ 3. Your parents set a good example by practicing responsible drinking behaviors.

_____ 4. Your family did not view drinking alcoholic beverages as a means of demonstrating maturity, adulthood, or masculinity/femininity.

_____ 5. Abstinence was accepted as a legitimate choice with respect to the consumption of alcoholic beverages.

_____ 6. Drunkenness was not an acceptable form of behavior.

_____ 7. Alcohol was viewed as a beverage and not as the central focus of a group activity.

_____ 8. The rules and rituals associated with drinking (as described in numbers 1 through 7 above) were known and understood by all group members; they were both reasonable and agreeable to those members.

Score (Number √'d)_____

The higher your score, the lower your risk of developing problems associated with drinking. Based on your score, what is your risk? Why do you believe this to be true?

HOW HEALTHY IS YOUR FAMILY?

Family life takes many forms. Some family characteristics are more functional and healthy than others. A healthy family environment provides for childrens' needs in a way that promotes normal emotional, physical, and social development.

For each of the following characteristics, circle **true** or **false** based on how well they describe your family.

<u>In my family:</u>

1.	All feelings are allright to express.	True False
2.	All subjects are open to discussion.	True False
3.	Individual differences are accepted.	True False
4.	Performance or what you do is more important than who you are.	True False
5.	Everyone must conform to the dominant person's ideas and values.	True False
6.	The atmosphere is generally tense.	True False
7.	Each person is responsible for his/her actions.	True False
8.	There are clear and flexible rules.	True False
9.	People feel loved and loving.	True False
10.	There are lots of "shoulds."	True False
11.	People feel tired and stressed.	True False
12.	Growth and change are discouraged.	True False

For each of the following answers, give yourself one point:

1.	true	4.	false	7.	true	10.	false
2.	true	5.	false	8.	true	11.	false
3.	true	6.	false	9.	true	12.	false

SCORING AND ANALYSIS

10-12 points   means you are very lucky to be part of a healthy and functional family.

4-9 points   means you have a family that tends to be functional but has some unhealthy characteristics.

1-3 points   means you have a family that is dysfunctional and unhealthy. Alcoholism, drug abuse, physical/sexual abuse may also be present. Professional help is seriously recommended.

Based on your perceptions of your family, answer the following questions:

1. Is your family healthy or unhealthy, functional or dysfunctional? Why or why not?

2. What dysfunctional characteristics are present in your family? How do these affect you personally? How might they be modified?

3. Children of dysfunctional families often become chemically dependent. Why do you think this happens?

C.A.S.T

Please check the answer below that best describes your feelings, behavior, and experiences related to a parent's alcohol or drug use. Take your time and be as accurate as possible. Answer all 30 questions by checking either "yes" or "no."

YES	NO		
_____	_____	1.	Have you ever thought that one of your parents had a problem with drinking or drugs?
_____	_____	2.	Have you ever lost sleep because of a parent's drinking or drug use?
_____	_____	3.	Did you ever encourage one of your parents to stop drinking or using drugs?
_____	_____	4.	Did you ever feel alone, scared, nervous, angry, or frustrated because a parent was not able to stop drinking or using drugs?
_____	_____	5.	Did you ever argue or fight with a parent when he or she was drinking or using drugs?
_____	_____	6.	Did you ever threaten to run away from home because of a parent's drinking or drug use?
_____	_____	7.	Has a parent ever yelled at or hit you or other family members when drinking or using drugs?
_____	_____	8.	Have you ever heard your parents fight when one of them was drunk or high on drugs?
_____	_____	9.	Did you ever protect another family member from a parent who was drinking or using drugs?
_____	_____	10.	Did you ever feel like hiding or emptying a parent's bottle of liquor or drugs?
_____	_____	11.	Do many of your thoughts revolve around a drinking or drug-using parent or difficulties that arise because of that parent's drinking or drug use?
_____	_____	12.	Did you ever wish that a parent would stop drinking or using drugs?
_____	_____	13.	Did you ever feel responsible for and guilty about a parent's drinking or drug use?

YES	NO		
_____	_____	14.	Did you ever fear that your parents would get divorced due to alcohol or drug use?
_____	_____	15.	Have you ever withdrawn from and avoided outside activities and friends because of embarrassment and shame over a parent's drinking or drug problem?
_____	_____	16.	Did you ever feel caught in the middle of an argument or fight between a drinking or drug-using parent and your other parent?
_____	_____	17.	Did you ever feel that you made a parent drink alcohol or use drugs?
_____	_____	18.	Have you ever felt that a problem-drinking or drug-abusing parent did not really love you?
_____	_____	19.	Did you ever resent a parent's drinking or drug use?
_____	_____	20.	Have you ever worried about a parent's health because of his or her alcohol or drug use?
_____	_____	21.	Have you ever been blamed for a parent's drinking or drug use?
_____	_____	22.	Did you ever think your father was an alcoholic or drug abuser?
_____	_____	23.	Did you ever wish your home could be more like the homes of your friends who did not have a parent with a drinking problem or drug problem?
_____	_____	24.	Did a parent ever make promises to you that he or she did not keep because of drinking or drug use?
_____	_____	25.	Did you ever think your mother was an alcoholic or drug abuser?
_____	_____	26.	Did you ever wish that you could talk to someone who could understand and help the alcohol or drug-related problems in your family?
_____	_____	27.	Did you ever fight with your brothers and sisters about a parent's drinking or drug use?

YES	NO		
_____	_____	28.	Did you ever stay away from home to avoid the drinking or drug-abusing parent or your other parent's reaction to the drinking or drug use?
_____	_____	29.	Have you ever felt sick, cried, or had a knot in your stomach after worrying about a parent's drinking or drug use?
_____	_____	30.	Did you ever take over any chores and duties at home that were usually done by a parent before he or she developed a drinking or drug problem?

_____ Total Number of **YES** Responses

A score of 6 or more indicates that, more than likely, you are the child of an alcoholic or drug-abusing parent. This may or may not come as a surprise to you. If you have concerns about the results of this questionnaire, please talk to your instructor or a counselor on your campus.

SOURCE: Instrument developed by John W. Jones, Ph.D. 1983. Camelot Unlimited, Chicago, Illinois.

 **WHAT CAN I DO?**

Now that you have completed the assessments of how alcohol and other drugs affect your relationships, you should have a better idea of the positive and negative effects of parental alcohol and drug use, and the attitudes and behaviors of friends and family members. Some questions to ask yourself at this point are:

Are my family and friends positive or negative influences

in my quest for a healthy lifestyle?

Do my family members and friends have alcohol

and drug-related problems, and how do these problems affect me?

What can I do if a family member or friend is in trouble

with alcohol and/or other drugs?

This skill-building section attempts to assist you in developing the thought processes and skills necessary to achieve a healthy perspective on the drug and alcohol use of your family and friends. Some of the skills addressed include handling peer pressure, identifying chemical dependence in family members and friends, learning about available resources, and how to intervene when someone you care about needs help.

BECOMING MORE ASSERTIVE

Assertiveness is behavior that enables you to act in your best interests, to stand up for yourself without undue anxiety, to exercise your rights without denying the rights of others. It is the direct, honest, appropriate expression of one's feelings, opinions, or beliefs. It shows consideration, but not deference, for other people. Assertive behavior communicates respect for the other person, but not necessarily the other person's behavior.

There are four behavioral components of assertive behavior:

1. Content

    A. In any assertive behavior, some specific goal is involved:
        1)   To establish a relationship with someone you want to know, or to change or end a relationship.
        2)   To express your feelings, beliefs, or opinions.
        3)   To state an objection or point of view in opposition to another.
        4)   To set limits for another person in regard to what can be expected or demanded of you.
        5)   To obtain something you want.

    B. Usually there are three basic components in the content of assertive behavior:
        1)   Recognition of the other person's feelings and rights (implicit or explicit)-"I realize you like such and such . . ."
        2)   Expression of your own feelings or rights—"however, I like so and so . . ."
        3)   Description of desired action—"therefore, let's . . ."

2. Eye Contact and Facial Expression

    A. The other person is more likely to respond to you if you look him or her in the eye.
    B. Appropriate expression lends credibility to assertion.

3. <u>Body Posture and Movement</u>

    A. The more relaxed you are, the more comfortable you'll feel asserting yourself, and the more successful you'll be.

    B. Turning away from the other person conveys a mixed message.

    C. Lowering your head conveys a mixed message usually.

    D. Appropriate hand gestures lend credibility.

4. <u>Vocal Tone and Quality</u>

    A. A fluid, rhythmic statement conveys more confidence than a low, halting voice.

In addition, there are a variety of assertive responses and assertiveness skills.

TYPES OF ASSERTIVE RESPONSES

1. <u>Assertive Talk</u>. Do not let others take advantage of you. Demand your rights. Insist upon being treated with fairness and justice. Examples: "I was here first." "I'd like more coffee, please." "Excuse me, but I have another appointment." "Please turn down the radio." "This steak is well-done, and I ordered it medium-rare."

2. <u>Feeling Talk</u>. Express your likes and dislikes spontaneously. Be open and frank about your feelings. Do not bottle up emotions. Answer questions honestly. Examples: "What a marvelous shirt!" "I'm tired as hell." "Since you asked, I much prefer you in another type of outfit."

3. <u>Greeting Talk</u>. Be outgoing and friendly with people whom you would like to know better. Do not avoid people because of shyness or because you do not know what to say. Smile brightly at people. Look and sound pleased to see them. Examples: "Hi, how are you?" "Hello, I haven't seen you in months." "What are you doing with yourself these days?" "How do you like working at ....?" "Taking any good courses?" "What's been happening with so and so?"

4. <u>Disagreeing Passively and Actively</u>. When you disagree with someone do not feign agreement for the sake of keeping peace by smiling, nodding, or paying close attention.

Change the topic. Look away. Disagree actively and emotionally when you are sure of your ground.

5.   Asking Why. When a person in power or authority asks you to do something that does not sound reasonable or enjoyable to you, ask why you should do it. You are an adult and should not accept authority alone. Request convincing explanations from teachers, relatives, and other authority figures. Make it understood that you will live up to voluntary commitments and be open to reasonable suggestions, but that you are not to be ordered about at anyone's whim.

6.   Talking About Oneself. When you have done something worthwhile or interesting, let others know about it. Let people know how you feel about things. Relate your experiences. Do not monopolize conversations, but do not be afraid to bring them around to yourself when it is appropriate.

7.   Agreeing with Compliments. Do not depreciate yourself or become flustered when someone compliments you with sincerity. At the very least, offer an equally sincere "thank you," or reward the complimenter by saying, "That's an awfully nice thing to say; I appreciate it." In other words, reward rather than punish others for complimenting you. When appropriate, extend compliments. For example, if someone says, "What a beautiful sweater!" respond, "Isn't it a lovely color? I had a hard time finding it."

8.   Avoiding Trying to Justify Opinions. Be reasonable in discussions, but when someone goes out of his or her way to dominate a social interaction by taking issue with any comments you offer, say something like, "Are you always so disagreeable?" or "I have no time to waste arguing with you," or "You seem to have a great deal invested in being right, regardless of what you say, don't you?"

9.   Looking People in the Eye. Do not avoid the gaze of others. When you argue, express an opinion, or greet a person, look him/her directly in the eye.

SOME ASSERTIVE SKILLS

The following skills may be helpful to you at times. You can choose which skills may be comfortable for you.

1. <u>Broken record</u> - This is a calm, persistent repetition of your feeling or need.

> "Could you lend me $50.00?"
> *"No, I'm not able to loan you the money."*
> "Please! I really need it!"
> *"It sounds like you're really desperate for the money, but I'm sorry. I can't help. What other possible ways of raising the money have you considered?"*

By using the "broken record," you can communicate your statement and may be able to work out a compromise that meets the needs of both you and your partner.

2. <u>Fogging</u> - This is acceptance of manipulative criticism by calmly acknowledging to your critic the <u>possibility</u> that there may be some truth in what he/she says. You remain your own judge. The effects of this are: 1) you can hear criticism without getting defensive; 2) the critical person may start listening to you and reduce his/her criticism.

> "You didn't seem interested in what I said."
> *"I can see how you may have gotten that impression."*

3. <u>Negative Inquiry</u> - This is the active prompting or soliciting of criticism in order to use the information (if helpful) or to exhaust it (if manipulative). This is also nondefensive and fosters communication.

> "I don't like your way of treating students."
> *"What is it about what I do that bothers you?"*

In this example, the person may learn about the impression others have of him or her, or about some mistaken information he/she has been giving out. The feedback may be helpful.

> *"I'm going out bowling."*
> "Why don't you stay home?!"
> *"I don't understand. What is it about my going out that bothers you?"*

This gives each person a chance to discuss their feelings and possibly reach an understanding. The response of "Why the hell shouldn't I go?" would only result in an argument.

4.   Negative Assertion - This is acceptance of your errors and faults (without apologies) by agreeing with constructive or hostile criticism. It enables you to be nondefensive and may reduce the other person's anger.

> "You did a lousy typing job."
> *"Yes, I did make some mistakes."*

It is important to remember that you must be the judge of your own behavior, and you should avoid passive agreement with unjust criticism.

5.   Free Information - This skill is learning to recognize simple cues given by a person that indicates what is important to them. When you pick up a cue in a conversation, you can ask the person about the subject and even mention your own feelings or experiences related to that subject.

> "I just moved here from Philadelphia."
> *"Oh, what brings you to D.C.? How do you like it so far?"*

You may want to add a comment about your own impressions of the area upon moving here, etc.

6.	<u>Self-Disclosure</u> - This skill involves accepting and initiating discussion of both positive and negative aspects of your personality, lifestyle, behaviors, etc., to enhance social communication.

> "I am worried about my ability to do this new job."
> *"I can understand that. I felt the same way when I started my last job. Is there something specific that worries you?"*

Here, not only have you provided some information about yourself for the other person to pursue, but you have also attempted to learn more about your new acquaintance.

WERE YOU ASSERTIVE?

Being appropriately assertive in any relationship is often difficult. When alcohol or drugs are involved, acting assertively and in your best interest may be challenging. The following scenarios focus on situations that may arise with family or friends.

Read each scenario and respond as if you encountered this situation. Then review the components of assertive behavior and skills to determine the assertiveness of your response to the scenario. After you have reviewed your responses, rewrite-using the components and skills-those responses which you feel were not as assertive as you would like them to be.

Scenario #1:

Although no one in your family has a problem with alcohol or drug abuse, alcohol is always served at every family gathering. You are uncomfortable with this and would like to suggest a change. How would you handle this?

Scenario #2:

During semester break, you are bringing home a new girlfriend/boyfriend who is currently in recovery from alcohol abuse. You want to discuss this with your parents before the visit and are concerned they will react poorly to this information. What will you say?

Scenario #3:

You currently live in the dormitory and are the only person of legal drinking age on your floor. Other students in the dorm are always asking you to buy alcohol for them, and usually you will do it. But, lately you are getting tired of this and do not want to buy alcohol for them anymore. What will you do?

Scenario #4:

Spring break is coming soon, and you have been invited to go to the beach with your friends. You have enough money to pay for your trip. However, you haven't been home since Christmas, and your parents feel you should spend your break with the family. You really want to go with your friends, and they are counting on you to help pay expenses. What will you do?

HANDLING PEER PRESSURE

Dealing with our friends and peers is often challenging. While most of us want to be liked, we also have to look out for our own best interests. Sometimes, we encounter situations in which asserting ourselves may put us in conflict with friends.

In this exercise read each scenario and respond to the accompanying questions.

Scenario #1:

You are 21 years old and work in a convenience store that sells beer and wine. No customers are in the store when some friends come in to see you. They are all under the legal drinking age. They want you to sell them some beer. You could get into serious trouble, even lose your job, for selling alcohol to minors, but your friends point out to you that nobody is in the store. What will you do?

Scenario #2:

You and your friends find a wallet with $100 and several credit cards in it. Your friends want to keep the money and return the credit cards, saying the wallet was found with no money. You have strong objections to this and believe everything should be returned. What will you do?

Scenario #3:

You and your roommate, who is your best friend, are driving home from a bar in your roommate's van. You have both been drinking, and your roommate is driving. You are stopped by a police officer. Your roommate is in a panic because he/she was arrested for DWI just two months ago. He/she pleads with you to switch seats before the officer approaches the car. It would be easy to do it, and he/she reminds you that you have never been arrested. What would you do?

Scenario #4:

Some friends are going to a campus rally to protest a new university policy. They are strongly opposed to it. You are in agreement with the policy and do not want to participate in the rally. What would you do?

QUESTIONS

1. Which scenarios were the most challenging for you? What made those scenarios difficult?

2. Are there other situations in which you deal with peer pressure? If so, how do you deal with them?

3. What would you like to change about your responses to your peers?

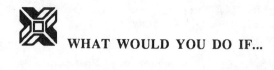 **WHAT WOULD YOU DO IF...**

Talking about drugs and drug use is not a difficult task, but doing something about drugs and drug use is more challenging.

What would you do if. . . .

1. Your best friend is using cocaine once or twice a week and frequently asks to borrow money from you to buy cocaine.

2. Your boyfriend/girlfriend is getting drunk three or four times a week and already has one DWI arrest, but continues to drink and drive.

3. You notice that your roommate is doing poorly in school, associates with people who sell drugs, and is becoming very moody.

4. Your girlfriend/boyfriend has been reading numerous magazine articles about "ecstacy" (MDMA) and becomes curious and wants to try it.

5. You arrive home from your sophomore year in college and find that your 13-year-old sister has started to smoke marijuana. She asks you not to say anything to your mom or dad, because she knows they would not approve.

6. You are at a restaurant enjoying a delicious dinner. As you are eating, you smell tobacco smoke, and it bothers you. You notice the man at the next table has finished his dinner and lit a cigar.

7. You arrive home for spring break, and the first night you are home, your father becomes very drunk and begins to yell obscenities at your little sister and beat up on your mother.

IS YOUR FRIEND IN TROUBLE?

Unfortunately, there may come a time when you are concerned about a friend's or family member's use of alcohol or drugs. Although you are not a professional who can offer a diagnosis, you have the advantage of observing that individual's behavior over time. Based on your observations, you may suspect a problem.

The purpose of this exercise is to provide you with a framework that may help you determine whether your friend or relative has a problem with alcohol or drugs. Read each statement carefully. If you believe a statement is true for the person for whom you are concerned, place a checkmark in the corresponding blank.

_____ your friend is young and feels strong
_____ uses alcohol or drugs out of curiosity
_____ uses them occasionally in a social setting
_____ functions well at school and home
Section A

_____ uses alcohol or drugs for pleasure
_____ uses drugs or drinks regularly at social events
_____ using makes him/her feel like he/she is one of the group
_____ any rebellious acts are within the range of normal adolescent behavior
_____ behavior in school remains stable
Section B

_____ your friend feels a need to drink or use drugs
_____ claims to be in complete control of alcohol and drug use
_____ uses drugs or drinks on a daily basis
_____ relationships with family and friends are becoming strained
_____ most of his/her crowd do drugs or drink
_____ devotes less time and attention to school work
_____ needs to drink or use drugs to feel better
Section C

_____ has lost control over alcohol and drug use

_____ needs to drink or use drugs to feel normal

_____ has had blackouts

_____ has not been taking care of his/her appearance, health

_____ may steal or commit other illegal acts

_____ tolerance to alcohol or specific drugs has increased

_____ uses drugs or drinks several times a day

Section D

_____ denies a problem with alcohol or drugs

_____ stops functioning completely at school, may even drop out

_____ becomes very depressed and may even contemplate suicide

_____ may have withdrawal symptoms once use of alcohol or drugs stops

_____ may blame others for his/her problems

Section E

SCORING AND ANALYSIS

Locate the section that has your last checkmark. If that check falls in:

Section A: Your friend is an experimental user.

Section B: Your friend is a social/recreational user.

Section C: Your friend is in the beginning stage of abuse.

Section D: Your friend is in the advanced stage of abuse.

Section E: Your friend is addicted.

Now that you have completed the checklist, please answer the following questions:

1. How might you approach your friend about his/her alcohol or drug problem?

2. Are there any other friends, family members, or significant persons who may be willing to work with you?

3. What kind of reaction do you anticipate?

4. What types of resources are available to you to help you prepare? What kinds of resources are available for your friend?

FIND OUT ABOUT SELF-HELP PROGRAMS

Many people have misconceptions about self-help programs, such as Alcoholics Anonymous (AA). One way for you to evaluate these groups is to attend an **open** meeting. Anyone who is interested in AA or Narcotics Anonymous (NA) is permitted to attend an open meeting. You do not have to be chemically dependent. Do not attempt to attend a **closed** meeting; these are only for individuals who are chemically dependent.

Anonymous group meetings are held just about everywhere, including college campuses. To find a meeting in your area, check your telephone directory for local listings and call:

Alcoholics Anonymous (AA) – a recovery program for those addicted to alcohol

Narcotics Anonymous (NA) – for those addicted to other drugs

Al-Anon – for those who are affected by a family member's use of alcohol

Nar-Anon – for those who are affected by a family member's use of other drugs

Adult Children of Alcoholics (ACOA) – for those who grew up in a home with a substance-abusing parent

Overeater's Anonymous (OA) – for compulsive overeaters

Gamblers Anonymous – for compulsive gamblers

IMPORTANT NOTE: When you attend a meeting, just listen, **do not** take notes, and be honest about why you are there.

1. What meeting did you attend? (type, location, time)

2. What were your expectations before you went to the meeting?

3. Were your expectations met? Were you surprised by anything you saw or heard?

4. Describe the format/activities that occurred during the meeting.

5. Describe the participants and the topics discussed without compromising their anonymity.

6. These programs are based on the 12 steps of Recovery. Describe these steps.

7. What was your personal reaction to the meeting? What did you think and how did you feel about what you observed?

8. Do you believe that these programs are effective? Why or why not?

WE'RE IN THIS TOGETHER

How do you define community? Your school, your neighborhood, or your city can each be considered a community. Can whole communities have problems with alcohol and other drugs? Does yours?

In a community, the members are bound together in some way. By virtue of this, communities usually have their own unique needs when it comes to the issues surrounding the use of alcohol and other drugs. Unfortunately, what works in one community will not always work in another, even if they are similar, and new strategies will need to be developed.

In the "community issues" section, students will be encouraged to experience creations of strategies by devising theoretical drug policies and educational programs to meet the needs of their community. The effects of media on the issues of alcohol and drug use will also be explored.

Lastly, the effects of alcohol and drug use on society will be presented. Students will be encouraged to examine both sides of an issue facing society today — the legalization of marijuana — and come up with their own opinions about this issue.

EXPLORING CAMPUS AND COMMUNITY CONTROVERSIES

Alcohol and drugs routinely show up in headlines and the media these days. In our society, controversy reigns over increased excise taxes on alcohol, penalties for drunk driving, and the potential legalization of currently illicit drugs. On college campuses, new policies on alcohol and drug use are being implemented. National chapters are placing tighter restrictions on alcohol consumption within fraternity and sorority houses, and some campuses are reconsidering regulations concerning alcohol use during rush activities. Images of alcohol use are ever present in television programming and advertising.

In this section, you will have the opportunity to examine issues facing universities and colleges as well as broader societal questions. By doing the exercises, you will be able to: 1) assess your attitudes about controversial issues, 2) explore the impact of alcohol and drugs on your campus, and 3) determine your level of knowledge of alcohol's effects on society. Your increased self knowledge on these relevant issues will assist you when, as a student and a citizen, you are called upon to make personal and political decisions about alcohol and drugs.

THE EFFECTS OF THE USE OF ALCOHOL AND OTHER DRUGS ON SOCIETY

Many times we forget that alcohol and other drug use can not only affect people on an individual level, but on a societal level as well.

The following questionnaire assesses what you know about the effects of alcohol and other drugs on society.

Circle the correct response to the following 30 questions.

---

1. About what percentage of American adults have a drinking problem?

   A. 5%

   B. 10%

   C. 30%

   D. Don't know

2. Which of the following is true about the drinking patterns of men and women?

   A. Men drink more than women.

   B. Men and women drink about the same amount.

   C. Women drink more than men.

   D. Don't know

3. About what percentage of American adults have no more than two drinks each week?

   A. 25%

   B. 65%

   C. 85%

   D. Don't know

4. Which of the following is true about children of problem drinkers?

   A. They are more likely than most other people to become problem drinkers.

   B. They have the same chance as other people of becoming problem drinkers.

   C. They are less likely than most other people to become problem drinkers.

   D. Don't know

5. Of the automobile crashes each year in which someone dies, about what percentage involve alcohol?

    A. 55%

    B. 75%

    C. 90%

    D. Don't know

6. About what proportion of violent crime (such as rape and assault) involves alcohol each year?

    A. Less than one-third

    B. Between one-third and two-thirds

    C. More than two-thirds

    D. Don't know

7. What is the approximate annual cost to society of problems caused by alcohol abuse?

    A. Hundreds of thousands of dollars

    B. Millions of dollars

    C. Billions of dollars

    D. Don't know

8. About what proportion of family violence (physical fighting) involves alcohol each year?

    A. About one-third

    B. About one-half

    C. About two-thirds

    D. Don't know

9. When the legal age for buying alcohol is lowered, what usually happens to the number of alcohol-related automobile crashes in which someone is killed?

    A. There is an increase in the number of fatal alcohol-related crashes.

    B. The number of fatal alcohol-related crashes remains about the same.

    C. There is a decrease in the number of fatal alcohol-related crashes.

    D. Don't know

10. About what percentage of Americans say that alcohol has caused a problem in their family?

    A. 10%

    B. 20%

    C. 30%

    D. Don't know

11. How often do marriages in which one or both partners have a drinking problem end in divorce?

    A. Less often than other marriages

    B. Equally as often as other marriages

    C. More often than other marriages

    D. Don't know

12. How does alcohol abuse compare to other diseases in terms of national health-care costs?

    A. Alcohol abuse is the second most costly medical problem.

    B. Alcohol abuse is the fifth most costly medical problem.

    C. Alcohol abuse is the tenth most costly medical problem.

    D. Don't know

13. On the average, how many times each day does a child in America see people drinking, i.e., alcoholic beverages on television?

    A. About 3 times a day

    B. About 8 times a day

    C. About 15 times a day

    D. Don't know

14. About what percentage of deaths from all diseases are related to alcohol use each year?

    A. 5%

    B. 10%

    C. 25%

    D. Don't know

15. When the price of alcoholic beverages goes up, what happens to the number of alcohol-related deaths?
    A. The number of deaths decreases.
    B. The number of deaths stays about the same.
    C. The number of deaths increases.
    D. Don't know

16. On the average, how many drinks do most American adults have each week?
    A. Less than 3 drinks
    B. About 5 drinks
    C. More than 10 drinks
    D. Don't know

17. About what proportion of violent crime (such as robbery and murder) involves the use of alcohol each year?
    A. Less that one-third
    B. Between one-third and two-thirds
    C. More than two-thirds
    D. Don't know

18. How do alcohol-related automobile crashes rank as a cause of death among teenagers?
    A. They are the #1 cause of death.
    B. They are the #2 cause of death.
    C. They are the #3 cause of death.
    D. Don't know

19. For every dollar Americans spend on alcoholic beverages, about how much money is spent to repair the damage caused by drinking?
    A. 50 cents
    B. 1 dollar
    C. 2 dollars
    D. Don't know

20. Of women who drink, about what percentage continue to drink while they are pregnant?

    A. 10%
    B. 40%
    C. 60%
    D. Don't know

21. Under a $2.9 million federal drug-fighting grant, members of the Texas National Guard:

    A. dressed up as cactus plants at night along the Mexican border in order to gather data on drug trafficking.
    B. invaded Colombia to destroy cocaine-manufacturing plants.
    C. patrolled the Gulf of Mexico in search of drug smugglers.
    D. were sent to Bolivia to train peasant farmers how to speak English.

22. The annual American market for illicit narcotics is:

    A. approximately equivalent to the federal budget deficit.
    B. twice what U.S. consumers spend for oil.
    C. about half the value of all U.S. currency in circulation.
    D. all of the above

23. The U.S. government spends more than $1 billion per year to stop drugs at our borders. According to the U.S. Coast Guard, what percentage of heroin and cocaine targeted for the United States is stopped at the borders through interdiction efforts?

    A. Approximately 37 percent
    B. Roughly 50 percent
    C. A little over 2 percent
    D. As little as 5 to 7 percent

24. The United States represents 5 percent of the world's total population. What percentage of the world's total volume of cocaine does the U.S. consume?

    A. Approximately 37 percent
    B. Roughly 50 percent
    C. A little over 2 percent
    D. As little as 5 to 7 percent

25. The Surgeon General recently reported that tobacco is as addictive as:

    A. heroin and cocaine.

    B. microwave popcorn.

    C. ice cream.

    D. soap operas.

26. According to information from the U.S. AIDS Commission, a primary reason for the spread of the HIV virus, (from which AIDS may be contracted) among the heterosexual population and newborn babies, is the lack of affordable, available drug-treatment programs for heroin addicts.

    A. True

    B. False

27. Coca, used in cocaine production, is grown at elevations of almost one-mile high throughout the rough terrain of the South American Andes mountain range. According to the Drug Enforcement Agency (DEA), what equivalent land area in South American does it take to grow enough coca to satisfy the United States' annual demand for cocaine?

    A. The state of Rhode Island

    B. A baseball field

    C. The borough of Queens, New York

    D. A K-mart parking lot

28. Working Americans with drug or alcohol problems are 25 percent less productive at their jobs than those without such problems. What percent of working Americans are impaired by some form of substance abuse?

    A. 15 percent

    B. 30 percent

    C. 20 percent

    D. 40 percent

29. Twenty-five percent of this group favors some form of decriminalization of marijuana?

    A. National Organization for Reform of Marijuana Laws (NORML)

    B. The drug gangs known as the Bloods or the Crips

    C. Colombian drug lords

    D. The nation's top chief prosecutors

30. At a cost of almost $100,000 to the taxpayer, 3,500 Customs Service employees were recently tested for illegal drugs. How many tested positive?

    A. 1
    B. 158
    C. 564
    D. 1,682

Correct Responses

1. b	11. c	21. a
2. a	12. c	22. d
3. b	13. b	23. d
4. a	14. b	24. b
5. a	15. a	25. a
6. c	16. a	26. a
7. c	17. c	27. c
8. b	18. a	28. a
9. a	19. c	29. d
10. c	20. c	30. a

SCORING AND ANALYSIS

Add up all your correct responses.

27 - 30   Good score! You are well informed on issues surrounding drug and alcohol use in society.

24 - 26   Give yourself a pat on the back; you are well aware of some of the negative effects alcohol and drug use can have on society.

21 - 23   Not bad; you are on your way to realizing the dangerous effects alcohol and drug use can have on society overall.

18 - 20   Needs some work; you are not fully cognizant of the impact of alcohol and drug use on our society.

Below 18   Time to get informed about some of the issues associated with drug and alcohol use in society.

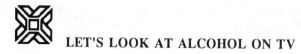

LET'S LOOK AT ALCOHOL ON TV

The use of alcohol is portrayed in television programming as well as in advertising. Although portrayal of alcohol use in soap operas, movies, sitcoms, and dramas reflects societal use of alcohol, it also influences our images and attitudes about alcohol use.

In this exercise, you are asked to watch five hours of television. It may be helpful to watch daytime soap operas as well as prime-time network programming. Write down the name of the program and its scheduled time. While you are viewing, consider these questions: Is the portrayal of alcohol use responsible or irresponsible? Is it realistic?

Name of show:	Time:

Was the portrayal of alcohol use responsible or irresponsible? Was it realistic? Please explain.

Name of show:	Time:

Was the portrayal of alcohol use responsible or irresponsible? Was it realistic? Please explain.

Name of show:	Time:

Was the portrayal of alcohol use responsible or irresponsible? Was it realistic? Please explain.

Name of show:	Time:

Was the portrayal of alcohol use responsible or irresponsible? Was it realistic? Please explain.

Name of show:	Time:

Was the portrayal of alcohol use responsible or irresponsible? Was it realistic? Please explain.

Now that you have thought about TV's portrayal of alcohol use, think about the following question: Should television be held accountable for responsible and realistic portrayals of alcohol use in its programming?

Now, your assignment is to write a letter to the president of a major network and advocate your position. If you believe television should be accountable, make suggestions of how the network might more effectively accomplish this task. If you do not believe television should be responsible for this, support your position.

DRUGS AND THE LAW

This survey has two parts. Both parts contain statements about possible consequences of being involved with illegal drugs.

In the first part, mark the column that best describes how likely you think it is that the consequence described would occur.

In the second part, mark the column that best describes how serious you think it would be if the consequence described occurred.

Part 1 - The Likeliness Scale

		Very Likely	Likely	Not Sure	Unlikely	Very Unlikely
1.	If you were arrested with cocaine in your possession, how likely is it that you would serve a jail sentence?	( )	( )	( )	( )	( )
2.	If you were convicted of a drug-related felony, how likely is it that you would lose the right to vote?	( )	( )	( )	( )	( )
3.	If you had an arrest record for possession of a small amount of drugs, how likely is it to harm your career?	( )	( )	( )	( )	( )
4.	If you were with friends when they were arrested for having drugs, how likely is it that you would be arrested as well?	( )	( )	( )	( )	( )
5.	If you frequently use a false ID to obtain alcohol, how likely is it that you would be arrested?	( )	( )	( )	( )	( )
6.	If you are driving while intoxicated, how likely are you to get arrested?	( )	( )	( )	( )	( )
7.	If you regularly used illegal drugs, how likely is it you would eventually end up in legal trouble?	( )	( )	( )	( )	( )

	Very Likely	Likely	Not Sure	Unlikely	Very Unlikely
8. If you were put on probation for a drug offense, how likely is it to cause serious problems in your life?	( )	( )	( )	( )	( )
9. If you were taken to court for a drug offense, how likely is it you would lose most of your friends?	( )	( )	( )	( )	( )
10. If you were arrested for a drug offense, how likely is it you would lose your job, even if you were not convicted?	( )	( )	( )	( )	( )

Part 2 - The Seriousness Scale

	Very Serious	Serious	Not Sure	Somewhat Serious	Not Serious
11. If you were convicted of possession of marijuana and given a fine and probation, how serious would it be?	( )	( )	( )	( )	( )
12. If you were given a one-year jail sentence as the result of a drug conviction, how serious would it be?	( )	( )	( )	( )	( )
13. If you lost your right to vote as a consequence of a felony drug conviction, how serious would it be?	( )	( )	( )	( )	( )
14. If you were questioned by police or school authorities about drug activities, how serious would it be?	( )	( )	( )	( )	( )
15. If you lost the right to travel outside of the United States as a consequence of a felony drug conviction, how serious would it be?	( )	( )	( )	( )	( )

	Very Serious	Serious	Not Sure	Somewhat Serious	Not Serious
16. If on job applications, you had to reveal a conviction for cocaine possession, how serious would it be?	( )	( )	( )	( )	( )
17. If you were prevented from getting a civil service job because of a drug conviction, how serious would it be?	( )	( )	( )	( )	( )
18. If police told your parents that you were associating with drug users, how serious would it be?	( )	( )	( )	( )	( )
19. If a member of your family had to get you out of jail following a DWI arrest, how serious would it be?	( )	( )	( )	( )	( )
20. If the police came to your house to ask about drug activities among your friends, how serious would it be?	( )	( )	( )	( )	( )

SCORING AND ANALYSIS

Separately score Part 1, the Likelihood Scale, and Part 2, the Seriousness Scale.

Part 1 - The Likelihood Scale

Point values are assigned to responses as follows:

Very Likely	= 5
Likely	= 4
Not Sure	= 3
Unlikely	= 2
Very Unlikely	= 1

Add up the point values of all your responses, and divide the total by 10. The maximum attainable score of 5 points indicates you perceive a high likelihood that negative legal consequences could result from illegal drug use. A mid-range score of 3 indicates you are unsure about the probability of negative legal consequences. A minimum score of 1 suggests you perceive a low likelihood that negative legal consequences could result from illegal drug use.

Part 2 - The Seriousness Scale

Point values are assigned to responses as follows:

Very Serious	= 5
Serious	= 4
Not Sure	= 3
Somewhat Serious	= 2
Not Serious	= 1

Add the point values of all your responses, and divide the total by 10. The maximum attainable score of 5 points indicates you perceive the potential consequences of illegal drug use to be very serious. A mid-range score of 3 indicates you are unsure about the seriousness of these consequences. A minimum score of 1 suggests you perceive the potential consequences of illegal drug use to be not serious at all.

ALCOHOL IMAGES IN THE MEDIA: GOOD OR BAD?

Alcohol advertising can be some of the most sophisticated advertising in the business. When watching an advertisement, a viewer may not realize that the product manufacturer is trying to portray a certain image of the product shown. But media advertisements and the images they portray have come under increasing scrutiny by the public.

The following exercise presents some issues in the debate over appropriate alcohol advertising at colleges and in society in general. What do you think? List both the pro and con sides of each issue presented. See if you can detect any patterns to your responses; if there are none, examine under what circumstances your opinions differ.

Alcohol Advertising at Colleges/Universities

Issue	Pro	Con
1. Sponsorship of college athletic events by alcohol beverage industry		
2. Alcohol advertising during televised college athletic events		
3. Spring break advertisements by alcohol companies		
4. Alcohol advertising in campus newspapers and on campus radio stations		

Alcohol Advertising in Society

Issue	Pro	Con
1. Alcohol advertising on television		
2. Use of attractive women in alcohol advertisements		
3. Use of sexual innuendo in alcohol advertising		
4. Public Service Announcements (PSAs) on responsible drinking by alcohol companies		

ADDITIONAL THOUGHTS

1. These are just some of the issues surrounding alcohol advertisements and images portrayed in the media. Describe two additional issues not mentioned here.

2. What are your major disagreements and/or concerns regarding the use of the media in alcohol advertising?

3. In your opinion, what restrictions should be placed on the alcoholic beverage industry regarding the marketing of their products on college campuses and in the media?

SOCIETAL MYTHS ABOUT ALCOHOL AND OTHER DRUGS

As a society, we hold various myths about alcohol and drugs as well as about their users. These myths are used to rationalize our behavior and support our inaction when we are confronted with an alcohol or drug-related problem. The following exercise is aimed at identifying common alcohol and drug myths, how these myths may be obstacles to action, and means of overcoming destructive myths.

Here are two examples of myths:

You cannot become an alcoholic drinking only beer.

Addiction to heroin is much worse than addiction to alcohol.

1. Identify a myth you hold about alcohol or drugs, their use, or the users.

2. What are the consequences of this myth for your campus? For your broader community?

3. How is this myth an obstacle to action that would alleviate or avoid any of the identified consequences?

4. How can this myth be overcome?

WHAT WORKS IN PREVENTION

There have been many approaches suggested that would respond to alcohol and drug use problems. Several of these are listed below.

How effective do you believe each of the following approaches have been in preventing alcohol and other drug use problems among college students?

		Not at all Effective			Very Effective	
1.	Develop a tough policy with severe penalties for anyone caught illegally using alcohol, tobacco, or other drugs.	1	2	3	4	5
2.	Make written materials on the dangers of alcohol, tobacco, and other drug use available to all students, faculty, and staff.	1	2	3	4	5
3.	Implement a year-round random drug testing program for students, faculty, and staff.	1	2	3	4	5
4.	Provide training for faculty and staff on the health, legal, and ethical risks of alcohol, tobacco, and other drug use.	1	2	3	4	5
5.	Provide opportunities for student groups (i.e., residence hall assistants, athletic teams, cultural groups, student government, etc.) to discuss guidelines for the use and nonuse of alcohol and other drugs.	1	2	3	4	5
6.	Provide opportunities for students to discuss the consequences of the health, legal, and ethical risks of alcohol, tobacco, and other drug use during freshman orientation.	1	2	3	4	5
7.	Provide student leadership training aimed at preventing alcohol and other drug use.	1	2	3	4	5

		Not at all Effective				Very Effective
8.	Provide students with instructions and practice in personal and social skills to resist pressures to use alcohol and other drugs.	1	2	3	4	5
9.	Assist students in planning and conducting alcohol- and drug-free activities.	1	2	3	4	5
10.	Conduct an annual alcohol awareness campaign on campus.	1	2	3	4	5
11.	Bring in celebrities and recovering chemically dependent speakers to describe the consequences of alcohol and other drug use to students, faculty, and staff.	1	2	3	4	5

QUESTIONS

1. Which of the prevention approaches do you believe would be most effective with college students and why?

2. Which of the prevention approaches do you believe would be least effective with college students and why?

3. What prevention approaches are currently being used on your campus?

4. What suggestions do you have for improving the prevention efforts on your campus?

Source: Adapted from *Policies and Programs for the 1990s.* 1990. Health Promotion Resources Consultants for U.S. Department of Transportation, U.S. Department of Education, and the U.S. Department of Health and Human Services.

HOW CAN I HELP?

After you have completed the assessments concerning the effects of alcohol and other drugs on your community, you should have a notion about the scope and nature of the alcohol and drug problem on our campuses, in our local communities, and in society at large.

What are the rights and responsibilities of students

regarding alcohol and drug use on campus?

What is the role of drug prevention and education in our society,

and does it work?

In the drug issue, which should take precedence,

individual rights or the public good?

This skill-building section attempts to assist you in developing the thought processes and skills necessary to achieve a comprehensive perspective on the problems of alcohol and other drug use in our society. Some of the skills addressed include assessing the impact of alcohol and drugs on your campus, developing problem-solving strategies to address drug and alcohol issues, and identifying existing and needed resources in your community.

ASSESSING THE IMPACT OF ALCOHOL AND DRUGS ON YOUR CAMPUS

The use of alcohol and drugs presents many challenges and dilemmas for every campus. Many campuses are considering new policies that may reflect a less permissive attitude. This exercise is designed to enable you to identify the impact of alcohol and drugs on your campus and to propose possible solutions for a problem you identify.

1.   Identify the impact and problems connected to the use of alcohol and drugs on your campus. Identify as many issues/problems as you wish.

2.   Prioritize your identified problems based on your assessment of their seriousness and importance.

3. Now choose one of those prioritized areas and go through the following steps:
   a) Give a specific and concrete definition of the problem.
   b) Who is impacted or affected by the problem?
   c) Who enables or perpetuates the problem?
   d) Who benefits from the problem?
   e) What are the obstacles to change?

4. Propose a specific solution for this problem.
   a) How would your solution be implemented?
   b) How would you evaluate its effectiveness?

DEVELOP A DRUG AND ALCOHOL POLICY FOR YOUR CAMPUS

> You have been nominated to serve on a committee established to formulate a campus drug and alcohol policy. In order to formulate this policy, you must answer the following questions.

1. Who will be affected by this policy?

2. What issues will be addressed in this policy?

3. What rules, regulations, and penalties will be included in this policy?

4. What will be the obstacles to acceptance of this policy on campus?

5. How will you evaluate the merit of this policy?

ALCOHOL AND DRUG ABUSE PREVENTION ON YOUR CAMPUS: WHAT DOES IT TAKE?

Prevention efforts take many forms on college campuses, from drug and alcohol education classes to legal sanctions for use and possession. Several levels of prevention are appropriate and necessary if a prevention program is to be comprehensive.

<u>Primary prevention</u> is directed at individuals who have not yet tried alcohol and/or other drugs. The goal of this program is the prevention of use.

<u>Secondary prevention</u> is directed at individuals who are experimental users of alcohol and/or other drugs. The goal of this program is the prevention of abuse and addiction.

<u>Tertiary prevention</u> is directed at individuals who are addicted or who are in recovery. The goals of this program are intervention/treatment and the prevention of relapse.

A comprehensive prevention program on a college campus may have several components, including:

A. Educational component-provides facts and information.
B. Affective component-deals with attitudes, beliefs, and feelings.
C. Skill-building component-develops competencies, such as assertiveness and decision making.
D. Social support component-provides a social support network of students, faculty, and staff.

If you were in charge of developing a comprehensive alcohol and drug abuse prevention program for your campus, what would you do? List your goals, the activities you would use to achieve those goals, and the groups you would target for these activities.

	GOALS	ACTIVITIES	TARGET GROUPS
1.			
2.			
3.			
4.			
5.			

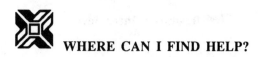 **WHERE CAN I FIND HELP?**

On your campus and within the broader community, numerous resources exist to assist those who may be concerned about their own or a family member's alcohol or drug use. However, until these resources are needed, we are often unaware of them. This exercise is designed to facilitate your awareness of community resources and foster an appreciation for the process of the individual who is seeking help for an alcohol or drug problem.

A list of potential resources/services on campus and within the community can be obtained through your campus health center, campus counseling center, residence-hall advisors, local health department offices, and the telephone directory under alcohol/drug addiction treatment services or mental health services. Once you have chosen a service, contact them by telephone to set up an appointment. By obtaining answers to the following items, you will have basic information about the services/resources. Feel free to ask other questions and note your questions with the responses on the following interview sheet.

Resource Interview

Agency/Office:

Address:

Phone:

Hours:

Contact Person:

Fees:

Services Offered:

Intake Procedure/How do you access services:

Agency Philosophy on Alcohol/Drugs:

Other Comments:

WHERE DO YOU STAND:
INDIVIDUAL RIGHTS VS. THE PUBLIC GOOD

In the United States, individual rights are protected by the Constitution and upheld by numerous Supreme Court decisions. Those individual rights include autonomy, protection of privacy, and freedom from undue governmental interference. In addition, policy decisions and governmental actions are also implemented to protect the public good. The public good is defined as the general health, well-being, and protection of the population. Occasionally, an issue presents itself which poses a conflict between individual rights and the public good. In the area of alcohol and drugs, several issues have emerged in recent years.

These issues include implementation of DWI laws, law enforcement and interdiction of illicit drugs, the legal drinking age, and drug testing of individuals. Choose one of these topics, and respond to the following questions.

Topic _____

1. What are the individual's rights in this case?

2. How is the public good defined in this case?

3. Is there a conflict between individual rights and the public good?

4. How would you resolve this conflict? Why have you chosen the options you've identified?

5 What are the social, economic, and legal costs and benefits of your decision?

Along with illicit drugs, we also use drugs which are beneficial; without some of these beneficial drugs life could be quite miserable. In the following exercise, imagine the following hypothetical situation: aliens have invaded the Earth and destroyed every drug known to humans.

List some of the advantages should this scenario occur:

Now list some of the disadvantages:

How did you go about making your decision? Did you find it difficult to distinguish whether some factors would be advantages or disadvantages?

Now pretend the aliens have decided that certain drugs would be allowed back into society. It is up to you to decide which drugs would be re-introduced. What drugs would you select and why?

SHOULD MARIJUANA AND OTHER DRUGS BE LEGALIZED?

After the Harrison Act went into effect, which made many drugs illegal, an illicit drug market appeared, and the cost of the illegal drugs increased dramatically. Recently, some prominent politicians have suggested that the legalization of drugs might reduce the crime rate and other associated social problems.

What is your view? Describe arguments for and against the legalization of marijuana and other drugs. These arguments may be personal in nature, scientific, or informed speculation.

Should Marijuana be Legalized?

Arguments for (positive effects)	Arguments against (negative effects)
1. Effects on individuals	1. Effects on individuals
2. Effects on families	2. Effects on families
3. Social consequences	3. Social consequences

4. Economic consequences	4. Economic consequences
5. Effects on the health-care system	5. Effects on the health-care system
6. Effects on the law-enforcement/criminal-justice system	6. Effects on the law-enforcement/criminal-justice system
7. Other effects	7.Other effects

Should Other Drugs be Legalized?
(including heroin, cocaine, LSD, etc.)

Arguments for (positive effects)	Arguments against (negative effects)
1. Effects on individuals	1. Effects on individuals
2. Effects on families	2. Effects on families
3. Social consequences	3. Social consequences
4. Economic consequences	4. Economic consequences

5. Effects on the health-care system	5. Effects on the health-care system
6. Effects on the law-enforcement/criminal-justice system	6. Effects on the law-enforcement/criminal-justice system
7. Other Effects	7. Other Effects

Based on your arguments for and against the legalization of marijuana and other drugs, answer the following questions:

1. Do you advocate the legalization of marijuana? Why or why not?

2. Do you advocate the legalization of other drugs, including heroin, cocaine, and LSD? Why or why not?

3. Do you feel the same about the legalization of marijuana and the legalization of other drugs? Why or why not?

LEGALIZATION OF MARIJUANA

The questions regarding the legalization and decriminalization of marijuana have been debated many times, so you will not be asked to debate that issue here. However, let us hypothetically assume that marijuana has recently been legalized in your state and you have been asked to set up guidelines governing the legality of marijuana. At your first press conference, how would you respond to the following questions?

1. At what age will it be legal for people to use marijuana and why?

2. Will marijuana be sold through special shops, such as liquor stores, or will it be available at supermarkets, drugstores, or convenience stores?

3. Penalties regarding driving and alcohol have not eliminated alcohol-related traffic fatalities. What would you propose to limit marijuana-related traffic fatalities?

4. What kind of penalties would you suggest for selling marijuana to minors?

5. Current law states that moonshine whiskey is illegal to produce. Would you prohibit the personal growing of marijuana?

6. Assuming marijuana legalization does not result in a tremendous increase in problems, would you favor legalizing other drugs such as cocaine, morphine, and LSD?

7. Would the smoking of marijuana be allowed in public places? Why or why not?

IN SUMMARY

Hopefully, with the completion of this workbook, you have become more aware and sensitized to the effects that alcohol and other drugs have on you personally, in your relationships, and in your community.

This final section helps you to synthesize and integrate the insights you have gained. The "Personal Reflections" exercise asks you to summarize what you have learned about yourself. The "Personal Risk for Addiction" questionnaire forces you to take a critical look at your potential for developing chemical dependence. Finally, the "Intentions" survey requires you to commit to paper your willingness to become actively involved in the struggle to overcome drug and alcohol problems in our society.

PERSONAL REFLECTIONS

Congratulations! You have completed *Making Choices.* You have given lots of thought to your own behavior, feelings, and thoughts; your relationships; and your views of the world around you. Based on the self-assessment exercises in *Making Choices,* it is time to summarize what you have learned about yourself.

The following series of questions have been designed to assist your integration and synthesis of what you have learned. Take your time and freely refer back through the exercises to help you respond.

1. Has your awareness of your alcohol/drug use changed? If so, how?

2. What factors have you identified as having an impact on your use?

3. Do you have any specific concerns about yourself or someone close to you? How will you address those concerns?

4. Assess your level of risk-taking behavior with regard to alcohol/drugs. Are you comfortable with your level of risk-taking? If not, how would you change?

5. Have you altered your ways of coping with stress or using your leisure time? If so, how?

6. Have any of your attitudes toward alcohol or drugs changed? If so, how have they changed?

PERSONAL RISK FOR ADDICTION

Based on your responses to the exercises in this workbook and your increased self-awareness, circle each of the following characteristics that you believe apply to you.

1. I use alcohol or other drugs on a regular basis.

2. I have experienced some negative consequences or problems as a result of my alcohol or drug use.

3. I have a family history (grandparent, parent, or sibling) of chemical dependence (including alcoholism).

4. I tend to have a compulsive personality.

5. I worry or feel bad about my alcohol or drug use.

6. I have friends who use alcohol or other drugs on a regular basis.

Score _____ (total number circled)

If you circled 2 or more of these items, you are at increased risk for addiction, as compared to the general public. It may be useful for you to seek the guidance of a counselor trained to assist with drug and alcohol problems. Please do not take the results of this lightly, it could mean your life.

INTENTIONS

All of us have a role to play in our society's struggle to overcome drug and alcohol problems. In some cases, our role is to focus on our own relationship with alcohol and other drugs. For others, it is dealing with the chemical dependence of a family member or close friend. Still others play a role in campus and community prevention and treatment efforts.

What is your role?

List below your intentions to get involved. You can get involved on a personal level, a relationship level, a community level, or all three.

On a personal level
I intend to ......

In my relationships
I intend to .....

On my campus
I intend to .....

In my community
I intend to .....

READ MORE ABOUT IT

Alcohol and Drugs

Carroll, C. R. 1989. *Drugs in Modern Society*. Dubuque, Iowa: Wm. C. Brown Publishers.

Duncan, D. & Gold, R. 1985. *Drugs and the Whole Person*. New York: Macmillan Publishing Company.

Gold, Mark S. 1984. *800-Cocaine*. New York: Bantam Books.

Gold, Mark S. 1986. *The Facts About Drugs and Alcohol*. New York: Bantam Books.

Johnson, Vernon E. 1986. *Intervention: How to Help Someone Who Doesn't Want Help*. Minneapolis: Johnson Institute.

Johnson, Vernon E. 1980. *I'll Quit Tomorrow*. New York: Harper & Row.

Kinney, J. & Leaton, G. 1983. *Loosening the Grip - A Handbook of Alcohol Information*. St. Louis: Mosby.

Moran, M. 1985. *Lost Years: Confessions of a Woman Alcoholic*. New York: Doubleday and Company, Inc.

Palfai, T. & Jankiewicz, H. 1991. *Drugs and Human Behavior*. Dubuque, Iowa: Wm. C. Brown Publishers.

Resnik, H. 1990. *Youth and Drugs: Society's Mixed Messages*. Rockville, Md.: Office of Substance Abuse Prevention, Department of Health and Human Services.

Rivinus, T. 1988. *Alcoholism/Chemical Dependency and The College Student*. New York: The Haworth Press.

Vaillant, G. E. 1983. *The Natural History of Alcoholism*. Cambridge, Mass.: Harvard University Press.

Waimon, L. A. 1987. *When Tears Don't Work*. Parsippany, New Jersey: Waimon Publishing, Inc.

Weil, A. 1986. *The Natural Mind: An Investigation of Drugs and the Higher Consciousness*. Boston: Houghton Mifflin Company.

Stress

Allen, R. J. & Hyde, D. H. 1988. *Investigations in Stress Control*. Edina, Minn.: Burgess International Group, Inc.

Benson, Herbert. 1975. *The Relaxation Response*. New York: Avon Books.

Brallier, Lynn. 1982. *Successfully Managing Stress*. Los Altos, Calif.: National Nursing Review.

Glasser, William. 1976. *Positive Addiction*. New York: Harper & Row.

Adult Children of Alcoholics

Black, C. 1981. *It Will Never Happen to Me.* Denver: M.A.C. Printing and Publication Division.

Cermack, Timmen L. 1988. *A Time to Heal: The Road to Recovery for Adult Children of Alcoholics.* Los Angeles: Jeremy P. Tarcher, Inc.

Larsen, E. & Hegarty, C. L. 1987. *Days of Healing, Days of Joy.* Center City, Minn.: Hazelden Educational Materials.

McConnell, P. 1986. *A Workbook for Healing.* San Francisco: Harper & Row.

Seixas, J. S. & Youcha, G. 1985. *Children of Alcoholism: A Survivor's Manual.* New York: Harper & Row.

Woititz, Janet. 1983. *Adult Children of Alcoholics.* Pompano Beach, Fla.: Health Communications, Inc.

Self-Help Books on Different Topics

Alberti, R. E. & Emmons, M. L. 1974. *Your Perfect Rights.* Impact Publishers.

Fensterheim, J. & Baer, J. 1975. *Don't Say Yes When You Want to Say No.* New York: Dell Books.

Kushner, Harold S. 1981. *When Bad Things Happen to Good People.* New York: Avon Books.

Lindquist, M. 1987. *Holding Back: Why We Hide the Truth About Ourselves.* New York: Harper & Row.

Norwood, Robin. 1985. *Women Who Love Too Much.* New York: Simon and Schuster.

ABOUT THE AUTHORS

Marjorie E. Scaffa is a doctoral candidate and an instructor in health education at the University of Maryland. She received a B.S. in psychology from the University of Maryland and an M.S. in occupational therapy from Virginia Commonwealth University in Richmond. She has worked in a variety of clinical settings, including the National Institutes of Health, with individuals addicted to alcohol and other drugs, and with their families. Currently, she teaches courses on drug and alcohol issues and is the director of a state-funded Alcohol/Drug Abuse Prevention Resource Center.

Sandra Crouse Quinn holds an M.Ed. in counseling from The American University, Washington, D.C. She has been employed as a therapist in substance abuse treatment programs, employee assistance programs, and in private practice. She designed and taught HLTH 498, Special Topics in Health: Personal and Community Perspectives on Alcohol and Drug Use, at the University of Maryland, College Park. Ms. Quinn is a doctoral student in health education at the University of Maryland.

Robert Swift is a health education teaching assistant and doctoral student at the University of Maryland. He received his B.S. from Ohio State University in 1980 and his M.Ed. in health education from the University of Virginia in 1986. He also earned an associate degree in respiratory therapy in 1983. He is currently teaching and working on research projects in the Department of Health Education at the University of Maryland. His areas of specialization include drug, alcohol, and sex education, and curriculum development.